Conquer Email Overload

Conquer Email Overload

WITH **Better Habits, Etiquette,** AND **OUTLOOK® 2007**

PEGGY DUNCAN

PSC
PRESS

ATLANTA, GEORGIA

Conquer Email Overload with Better Habits, Etiquette, and Outlook 2007
Published by
PSC Press
1691 Phoenix Blvd, Suite 380
Atlanta GA 30349
404-492-8197
www.ConquerEmailOverload.com

©Copyright 2010 by PSC Press, Atlanta, Georgia. All rights reserved.
No part of this book may be used or reproduced in any form or by any means, or stored in a database or retrieval system via any medium, without prior written permission of the publisher, except in the case of brief quotations embodied in articles and reviews.

ISBN-13: 978-0-9674728-7-4

Library of Congress Control Number: 2010905712

Manufactured in the United States of America

Visit the book's Web site at www.ConquerEmailOverload.com.

Book created in Microsoft® Word. Author photo by Philip McCollum Photography, Atlanta, GA (www.MccPhoto.com). Cover design by Sandy Barth, www.HighProfileStudio.com.

Trademarks
Outlook, Bing, and Microsoft are registered trademarks of Microsoft® Corporation. Screen shots reprinted by permission from Microsoft Corporation. Any other trademarked products mentioned belong to their respective companies.

Data used in screens and sample output is fictitious unless otherwise noted.

Lizzie

Acknowledgments

Many thanks again to my family members who understand how I am when I go into my shell to write. Mom calls to remind me to exercise. Maurice makes sure I eat well and drink plenty of water. And my son, Steven, calls just to say "Hey Ma. Whatcha doin'?" I appreciate you all so much.

When I needed another set of eyes to check this book, I asked for help from people on my private email list. What a team! Their helpful suggestions and painstaking review of my logic and instructions made this a much better book. Thank you!

Review Panel
Beverley Bennett, Office Administrator, Liberty Mutual Management (Bermuda) Ltd.
Carolyn B. Pund, CMP, CMM, Global Meetings & Events Manager
Jacquee Minor, Business Writer, J Minorlogues
Juanita McDowell, President and Owner, InMotion Real Estate Institute
Lila Baschieri CPS/CAP, Executive Assistant, Pitney Bowes Management Services
Pollie Massey Battle, Diversity Leadership Consultant, OMS Consulting & Training, Inc.
Suzette Eaddy, CMP, Director of Conferences, National Minority Supplier Development Council

Special Assistance
Glenda Moss, Support Specialist, Anderson Communications
Vicki Nutter, Support Specialist, Georgia Power

Contacting the Author

If you have a request, comment, or testimonial for this book, Peggy looks forward to hearing from you.

Connect at worksmart@PeggyDuncan.com or call 404-492-8197 Eastern.

www.DigitalBreakThroughs.com
The Digital Breakthroughs Institute
Atlanta GA
Technology and Productivity Training Open to the Public
Founder, Peggy Duncan

www.PeggyDuncan.com
Join Peggy's Private Email List
Receive timesaving tips and free eNewsletter

www.SUITEMinute.com
Peggy's Award-Winning Technology Blog
Technology tactics that make work easier

www.Facebook.com/DigitalBreakThroughs
Facebook Fan Page - Join for free

www.Twitter.com/peggyduncan
Follow Peggy on Twitter

www.YouTube.com/digitalbreakthroughs
YouTube Channel with How-To Videos

Raving Fans

> I love the way you find new tricks that I never would have had the time to discover on my own.
> **Carolyn Pund, CMP, CMM**
> Global Meetings & Events Manager

> You have captured so many good tips in this book that I can actually use every day.
> **Lila Baschieri CPS/CAP,** Executive Assistant
> Pitney Bowes Management Services

> I'll keep my eye out for other speaking engagements for you! I don't do this for just anyone....you are just so amazing I want to share you with everyone I know!
> **Linda Bruns,** National Sales Manager
> Shepard Exposition Services

> I just heard you in San Jose - you are amazing - I wish you would have talked all week.
> **Nova Simpson**

> I continue to be amazed by what Outlook can do and your book presents the information in terms that everyone can understand.
> **Suzette Eaddy, CMP,** Director of Conferences
> National Minority Supplier Development Council

> I learned more in one sitting from Peggy's book than I did in the entire five months that I've been using Outlook 2007. This book gave me practical, useable advice on how to simplify my life.
> **Pollie Massey Battle,** OD Consultant, President
> OMS Consulting & Training, Inc.

> I love the way you've blended your skills as a time management expert with Outlook.
> **Juanita McDowell,** President and Owner
> InMotion Real Estate Institute

CONTENTS

OUTLOOK'S NEW LOOK 2
Ribbon Basics 2
- Office Button 3
- Dialog Box Launcher 3
- Quick Access Toolbar 4
- Mini Toolbar 4
- Browse the Web from Outlook 4
- To-Do Bar 5

DO THIS FIRST 6
Navigation Pane 6
- Create a Shortcuts Navigation Pane 8
  - Add a Shortcut to an Outlook Folder 9
  - Add a Shortcut to a Windows Folder 9
Reading Pane 9
Toolbars 9
Create File Structure 10
- Naming Mail Folders 10
- Separate Messages Into Folders 10
  - Create a CYA Folder 11
- Copy a Set of Folders 11
Return to Inbox 12
Create a Default Signature 13
- Create Different Signatures for Each Email Account 14
- Switch Signatures Inside a Message 15
Create Repetitive Responses 16
- Quick Parts 16
- Use Signatures for Responses 17
- Create the Message and Save as msg 17
- Create a Template for Your Message 18
  - Delete a Template 18

    Create an Autoresponder 19
  Customize Word's Quick Access Toolbar 20
  Turn On Spelling Check 22
    Custom Dictionary 22
  Sync Other Email Accounts to Outlook 22

EMAIL - MANAGE MESSAGES 23

Change How You Use the Inbox 23
  Best Time to Check Email 24
  Establish a Routine 25
    Email Addict 25

Methods for Clearing the Inbox 26
  First Method: Eliminate Junk Email 27
    Change How Junk Email Gets Filtered 28
    Move Messages from Junk E-mail Folder 28
    Empty Junk E-mail Folder 29
    Add to Blocked Senders List 29
      Oops! Delete from Blocked Senders List 30
    Use Signature Line to Discourage Junk 30
    Ask People You Know to Stop Sending Junk 30
    Add to Safe Senders List 31
    Create a Disposable Email Address 31
    Cloak Your Email Address on the Web 32
  Second Method: Redirect Messages with Rules 32
    Color-Code Messages from Certain Senders 32
    Send Messages to Special Folder 33
    Move Messages With Certain Subject Line 34
    Change a Rule 34
  Third Method: Separate Inbox Messages with Categories 35
    Create a Category 37
    Assign a Category 37
      Set Quick Click 38
    Change a Category 38
    Remove a Category 38
    Create a Rule for a Category 38

Fourth Method: Flag Messages for Follow-Up 41
Flag Without a Reminder 41
Flag With a Reminder 41
Set Quick Click for Reminders 42
Adjust Time for Default Reminder 42
Remove a Flag 42
Flag Outgoing Messages for Follow-Up 42
Flag Message for Your Benefit 43
Flag Message for Recipients to See 43
Flag Message with Reminders for You and Recipient 44
Respond to Flag with Delete, Complete, or Clear 44
Hide Flagged Messages 44
Fifth Method: Filing the Keepers 45

Find Messages Fast 45
Instant Search Box 45
Rebuild the Search Catalog 47
Find Messages Addressed to You 48
Find Unread Messages 48
Find Messages With Attachments 48
Find Messages from a Sender 48
Find Related Messages 49
Find Messages by Conversation Topic 49
Define Your Own Views 49
Search Folders 49
Default Search Folders 50
For Follow Up Search Folder 50
Create More Search Folders 50
Build Your Own Search Folders 51
Create a Search Folder for a Category 52
Change a Search Folder 53
Delete a Search Folder 53
Advanced Find 53
Sort Messages 54
Field Chooser 54
Arrange By 55
Sort Messages by More Than One Column 55

Customize Current View 56
Group By Box... 56

Messages You RECEIVE.. 56
Adjust the New Message Alert 56
Turn Off the Ding.. 57
Keep Read Messages Bold 58
Define Large Messages... 58
Block Automatic Download of Pictures.. 59
Deleting Messages.. 60
  Deleted Items Folder 60
  Delete from the Deleted Items Folder 61
  Recover Deleted Items 61
Editing Messages 61
  Edit Subject Line 61
  Edit a Message Before You File It 62
Saving Messages... 62
  Save a Message Outside of Outlook 62
  Save Multiple Messages as One File 62
  Keep Messages on the Server 63
Printing Messages 64
  Print Portion of a Message 64
Use Out of Office Email Feature 64
Subscribe to RSS Feeds 65

Messages You SEND 65
Create Better Messages.. 65
  Grammar Rules Apply 68
  Add Interest to Your Message with HTML............................... 69
  Decorations: Designs, Emoticons, and Smileys 70
  Use a Typeface that Fits 70
  Improve the From Line 71
  Email Pet Peeves 71
  What Not to Send Via Email 75
Improve Your Image... 76
  The Right Email Address... 76
  Email Etiquette 77

xvi

Send a Message to a Contact 78
   Use an Email Address that Pops Up 78
   Delete Email Addresses that Pop Up on To Line 78
   Send a Message to Multiple People with Bcc 79
   Send a Message from the Contacts Folder 79
Send a Message to a Category 80
Send a Message to a Distribution List 82
Send Personalized Email Messages 82
   Mail Merge to All Contacts 82
   Mail Merge to a Category 83
   Mail Merge to Selected Contacts 84
Change Delivery Options 84
   Delay Delivery of All Messages 84
   Delay Delivery of a Single Message 87
   Direct Replies to Someone Else 88
Flag a Message You Send 88
Insert Items into a Message 88
   Insert Your Calendar 88
   Insert a Picture 89
   Insert Objects (Word Table, Excel Spreadsheets, Shapes) 89
      Paste Special and Link to Original Data 89
   Insert Message Into Other Items 90
Reply to Messages 90
   Create and Save Text You Use Often 92
Forward Messages 92
   Get Rid of Carets (>> <<) 92
Resend a Message 93
Save Copy of Sent Messages to Different Folder 94
Recall a Message You Just Sent 94
Determine What You've Done with a Message 95
Sending Large Files or Folders 96
   Email Entire Folder 96
   Send Huge Files and Folders Via the Internet 96
Voting 96
   Add Voting Buttons to a Message 97
   Process Voting Responses 97

Tally and Sort Votes 98
Cast Your Vote 98

Managing Attachments 98
Receiving Attachments 98
Open or Preview Attachments 98
Save Multiple Attachments 99
Find Messages With Attachments 99
Sending Attachments 99
Add an Attachment to the Message 99
Resize Attached Picture Before You Send 100
Add Attachments from Your Taskbar 100
Attach a Virtual Business Card (vCard) to a Message 102

TASKS - TRACK AND REMEMBER WORK 103

Processing Tasks from the Inbox 103

Create a Task 106
Create a Task from Scratch 106
Turn an Email Message Into a Task 106
Turn a Calendar Appointment into a Task 107
The Task Window 107
Add Categories to a Task 109
Change How You View Tasks 110
Customize How Tasks Appear on the To-Do Bar 111
Show Only Today's Tasks on To-Do Bar 112
Create Recurring Tasks and Reminders 112
Stop a Recurring Task 113
View the Task Timeline 113
Closing Out a Task 113
Delete Completed Tasks (or Not) 113

Delegate a Task (Task Request) 113
Create a Task Request from Scratch 113
Stop or Redirect Task Updates 114
Send a Task Request to Multiple People 114

Attach an Email Message to a Task Request	115
Attach a File to a Task Request	115
Create a Task Request from Contacts	115
Turn a Message You're Creating into a Task Request	115
Create a Task Request from a Message You Received	116
Create a Task Request from Existing Task	116
Cancel a Task Request	116
Track Tasks You Have Delegated	116
Reclaim a Rejected Task Assignment	116
Send Comments About Delegated Work	116
Receive Task Requests	**116**
Accept or Decline a Task Request	116
Update List	117
Track Time Spent and More	117
Send Status Report	117
Schedule Time for the Task	117

CALENDAR - STAY ON SCHEDULE 118

Calendar Management	**119**
Principles of Calendar Management	119
Setting Up Your Calendar for Work	120
Create Text and Color Formatting	120
Change Calendar Views	121
Date Navigator	121
Define Your Own Views	122
Use Dual Monitors and Expand Your Desktop	126
Change Calendar Options	126
Mark Appointment Private	126
Add Holidays	127
Change Workweek	127
Change Time Zone	127
Change Time Scale	127
Creating Additional Calendars	127
Viewing Additional Calendars – Calendar Overlay	128
Sharing Your Calendar	129

Send Your Calendar Via Email 129
Printing a Calendar 129
   Customize the Print Style 129
   Resetting the Print Style 131
   Choosing What to Print 131
   Print a Blank Calendar 132
Calendar Reminders 132
   Change Default Reminder 132
   Talking Alarm Clock 132

Scheduling (Appointments, Meetings, Events) 133
Create an Appointment 133
   Create an Appointment from Scratch 133
      Use Text in Your Outlook Date and Time Fields 133
      Add Map and Driving Directions 134
      Link with Contact 134
      Add Categories 134
      Automatic Formatting 135
   Create a Recurring Appointment 136
   Change Appointment Date or Time 137
      Copy Appointment to Another Day 137
      Move Appointment to Another Day 137
   Create an Appointment from the Inbox 137
Create and Send a Meeting Request 140
   Check Other People's Schedules 142
      Scheduling Assistant 142
      AutoPick Next 143
      Group Schedules 143
         Create a Group Schedule 143
         Use a Group Schedule 143
      Schedule Resources 144
         Turn Off Automatic Acceptance of Meeting Requests 145
Track Responses to Meeting Requests 145
Update a Meeting Request 145
Cancel a Meeting 146
Send a Meeting Request to a Distribution List 146
Receiving a Meeting Request 146

Create an Event 147
Find Calendar Appointments Fast 147

CONTACTS - STAY CONNECTED 148

Create Contacts – Your Outlook Database 148
   Add Multiple Phone Numbers and Addresses 149
   Add Contact Photo 150
   Add People to Contacts from Inside a Message 150
   Linking Contacts 151
   Categorize Your Contacts 151
      Add Categories to New Contacts 152
      Add Categories to Current Contacts 152
      Remove a Category from a Contact 152
      View Contacts by Category 152
   Other Uses for Contacts 152
   Export All Contacts 155
   Export Some Contacts 155
   Remove Duplicates in Outlook 155

Find a Contact 155
   Group By Box 156
   Find a Contact Within a Message 157
   Add Notes to a Contact and Find Later 158

Flag a Contact for Follow Up 158

Create Distribution Lists 159
   Create a Distribution List from Names in Message 159
   Create a Distribution List from Contacts 160
   Create a Distribution List from Scratch 161
   Update a Distribution List 161
      Remove a Name from a Distribution List 161
   Find a Distribution List 162
   Send a Message to a Distribution List 162
      Expand Distribution List and Delete Names 162
      Send Email Addressed to Undisclosed Recipients 163

Send a vCard or Distribution List 164
Send Distribution List to Another User 164
   Save a Distribution List or vCard You Receive.............................. 165
Move a Distribution List to a New Computer 165
Print a Distribution List 165

NOTES – USE TO REMEMBER 166

Create a Note 167

MAINTENANCE 168

Archive 168
   AutoArchive Instead of Deleting 168
   Archive Files Manually 169
   Find Archived Files 169

Back Up Your Data 169
   Check Folder Sizes 169
   Back Up (Almost) Everything at Once (.pst) 170
      Back Up Your Rules 171
      Back Up Quick Parts 171
      Move Quick Parts to a Different Computer 172
      Back Up Signatures 172

STAY OUT OF TROUBLE 173

Company Email Policy 173
   Simple Email Policy 174
   Extensive Email Policy 175

Introduction

Outlook is like the cockpit of an airplane. Just about anything you need to do at work can be managed from it.

Overview of the Chapters

First, you'll learn how to move from one message to the next, finish quickly, and free up more time for other important projects. Next, you'll explore Tasks and how to manage and remember work you do every day. After that, you'll use Calendar to stay on schedule. Then, you'll move to Contacts and stay connected with everyone in your network. To help you keep up with tidbits of information you may have scattered everywhere, you'll learn how to use electronic notes and integrate them throughout Outlook. Next, you'll discover maintenance tips for keeping Outlook running smoothly. And finally, you'll incorporate an email policy for your organization that will keep you out of trouble. And mixed throughout all of this are time management principles I use every day.

Writing Style

You won't see any fluff in this book. I have a habit of not taking ten pages to express something I can say in a paragraph. You'll notice throughout this book that I get right to the point. If the heading explains what the text is about, I don't waste words re-explaining it. When it's obvious that you need to click OK until you're back out of a dialog box, I don't say it.

Formatting

I've done my best to keep the formatting consistent throughout this book. When you have to click, the text is bold except when I offer an alternative method. When I refer to a section of a dialog box, it's in *italics*.

How to Learn Outlook

The best way to learn Outlook is to start from the beginning chapter and work your way through the book. Do this whether you think you already know something or not. There are wonderful nuggets throughout, and I don't want you to miss any.

Right now, you may feel that you're out of control. All of this is about to change if you commit to going through the tips and tricks outlined in this book. So go ahead and get comfortable, clear the calendar, close the door, and start learning how this powerful software can solve life's problems!

OUTLOOK'S NEW LOOK

Ribbon Basics

With Office 2007, Microsoft has changed some of the look and feel of Outlook. In some views such as New Message or New Appointment, you'll notice the traditional menus have been replaced by what is now called a Ribbon. It has three main parts: tabs, command buttons, and groups.

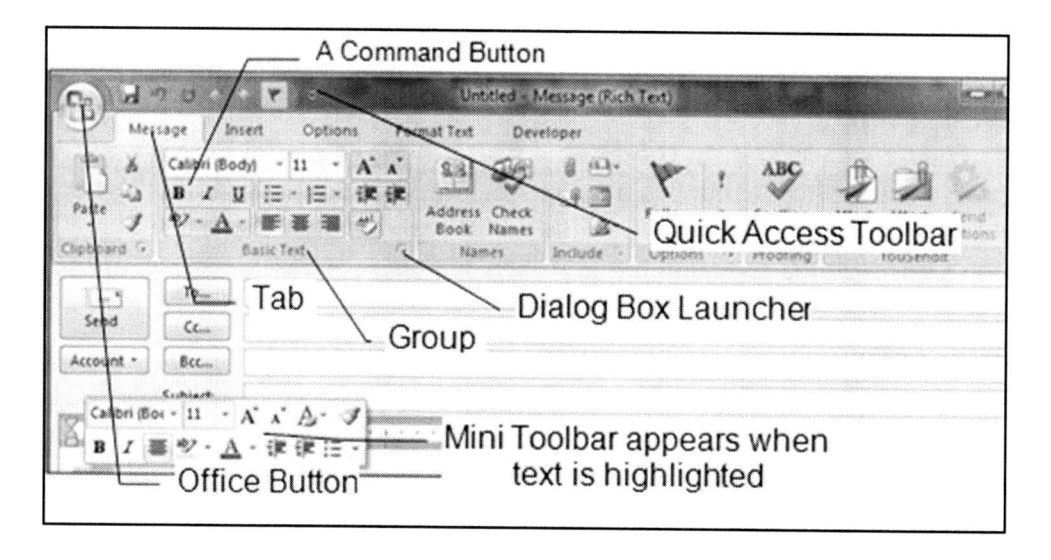

Figure 1. Study these new components as they're mentioned throughout this book.

1. **Tabs.** Tabs represent the main sections of the Ribbon. Each one leads to a variety of related commands that change based on which folder you're in.

2. **Command Buttons.** Individual actions such as cut or paste happen when you click a command. To see all commands at a glance, your window should be maximized.

3. **Groups.** Related commands are separated into groups on each tab. For example, when you create a new message, you'll see the text editing commands together inside the Basic Text group on the Message tab.

Office Button

The File menu has been replaced by the Office button. When you're in a window and you see this button, you can click it to create a new Outlook item such as Meeting, Appointment, etc.

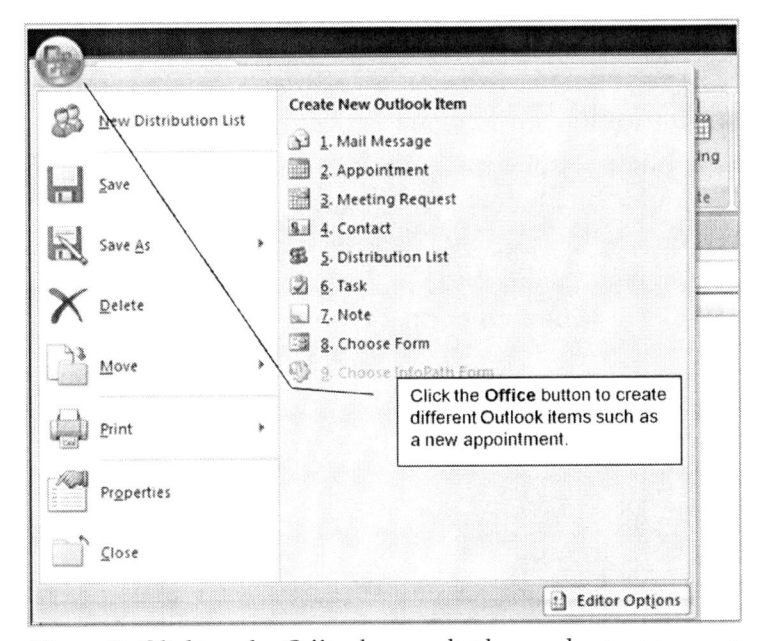

Figure 2. Clicking the Office button displays a shortcut to create a new item.

Dialog Box Launcher

Many commands are not visible by default. Some groups have the Dialog Box Launcher (the little arrow in the corner under a group). When you click it, you'll gain access to other commands related to what you're trying to do (refer to Figure 1 on page 2).

| 3

Quick Access Toolbar

The Quick Access Toolbar is a customizable toolbar located next to the Office button (you'll see it when you're in a view that shows tabs). When you want quicker access to a command, you can customize this toolbar and add it here. This toolbar operates independently of the active tab and can be moved from above the Ribbon to below. (Refer to Figure 1 on page 2. Click the Customize Quick Access Toolbar button, and click **Show Below the Ribbon**.)

📢 *For step-by-step instructions on how to customize this toolbar, see page 20.*

Mini Toolbar

When you select text then point to it with the mouse, the Mini Toolbar appears. Hold the mouse pointer over it to bring it into focus. You can make changes to the selected text by clicking any command on it (refer to Figure 1 on page 2).

Browse the Web from Outlook

This isn't a new feature, but a lot of people don't know that you can browse the Web while you're in Outlook. You'll need to display the Web toolbar (right-click on any toolbar, and click **Web**). Once the toolbar is displayed, type the Web address in the Address Box, and press **Enter**. Later, click the **Back** button until you're back to normal view (or click a folder).

Figure 3. You can browse the Web from Outlook. From any main folder view such as Mail, right-click on any toolbar, and tick to display the **Web** *toolbar.*

To-Do Bar

New to Outlook 2007 is the To-Do Bar. It displays the Date Navigator (more on this in the Calendaring chapter), upcoming appointments, task input box, and a task list of flagged messages (more details on this later). Appointments marked "Private" appear with a lock icon. Once displayed, the To-Do Bar is always in view (if you don't see it by default, press **Alt+F2** or click the **View** menu, **To-Do Bar, Normal**).

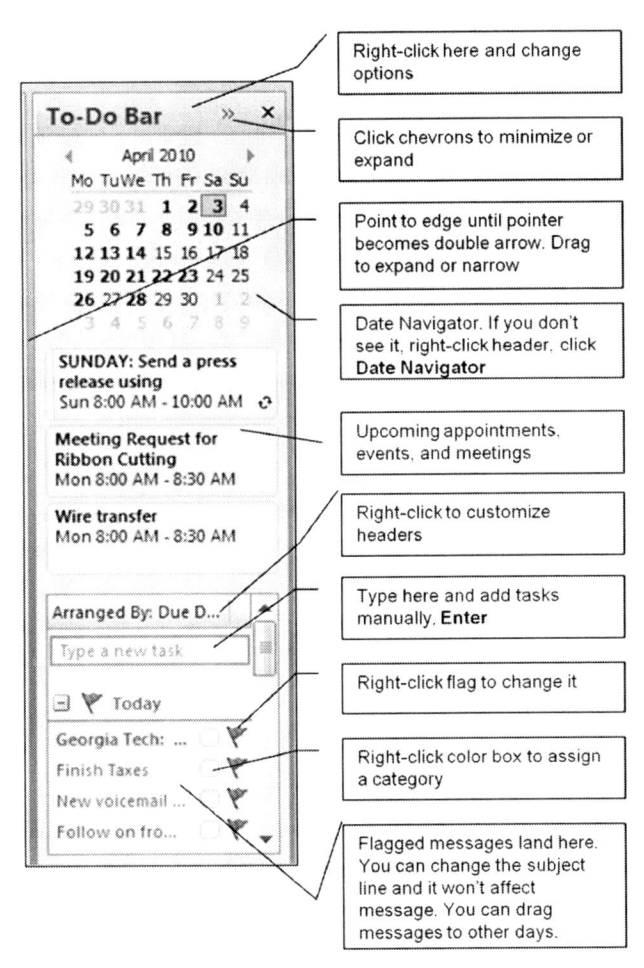

*Figure 4. Messages that you flag for follow up and anything you add to Tasks appear here automatically. Avoid dragging messages here because if you delete it from here, it's deleted everywhere (drag to Tasks instead). The perfect way to keep up with your daily tasks is by typing them directly in the **Type a new task** box.*

DO THIS FIRST

STEP 1 Change how you view Outlook items so the instructions in this book match what you'll see.

Navigation Pane

You can change how you view Outlook that fits the way you work. For now, make the following adjustments so what you see matches the instructions in this book. You can change everything again later.

Open Outlook and go to the **Mail** folder (Inbox view). You should see the Navigation Pane on the left. It contains access to the Calendar, Contacts, Deleted Items, Drafts, Inbox, Notes, Outbox, Sent Items, and Tasks. If you don't see it, click the **View** menu, **Navigation Pane**.

When dragging items from one item to the next, say from your Inbox to the Calendar, you can drop it on a folder in the Navigation Pane and turn one type of item into another (this is called AutoCreate).

You can quickly switch among various Navigation Panes with these shortcuts: CTRL+1 Mail, CTRL+2 Calendar, CTRL+3 Contacts, CTRL+4 Tasks, CTRL+5 Notes, CTRL+6 Folder List, CTRL+7 Shortcuts, CTRL+8 Journal.

The Navigation Pane for the Mail folder is divided into four panes.

- **Favorite Folders**. These are the Outlook folders you refer to often and want quick access to. If you don't see them, click the **View** menu, **Navigation Pane, Favorite Folders**. If you want to add to this section, click the desired folder and drag it here (or right-click the desired folder, and click Add to Favorite Folders).

- **Folder List (Mail Folders).** This section houses all your Outlook folders. You can display this list in any view by clicking the Folder List icon (unlike the other icons in the Navigation Pane, clicking it does not change the folder. When you click to open a different folder, it disappears).

- **Current View.** Default views have been created that provide a quick way to change how the current folder is organized. If you don't see this pane, click the **View** menu, point to **Navigation Pane**, click **Current View** (if collapsed, click the chevrons (^) to show more. Later, you'll create your own views that will appear here.

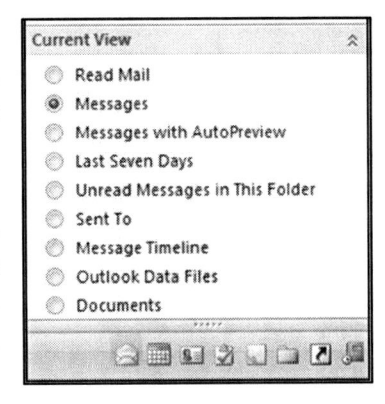

- **Item Icons.** You can get to all Outlook items in the bottom section of the Navigation Pane by clicking the desired icon. You can customize what you see also (refer to callouts in the figure).

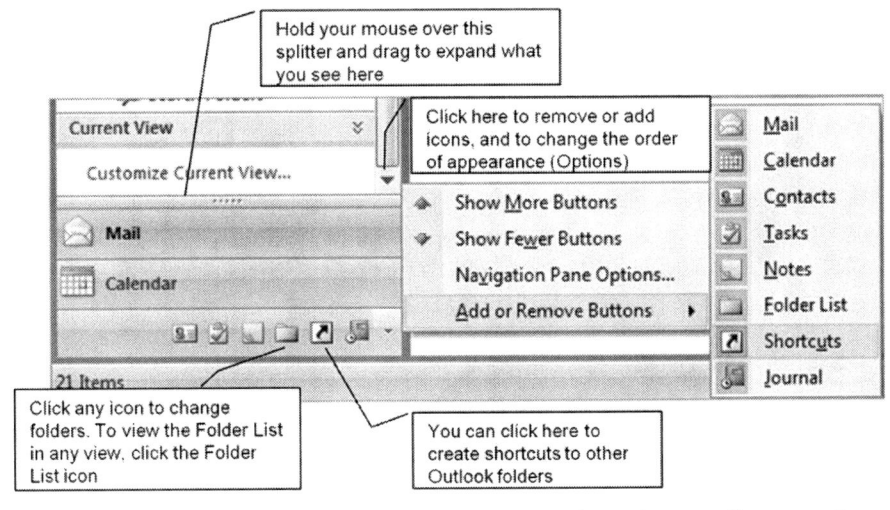

Figure 5. The Navigation Pane can be customized. Refer to callouts in this figure.

Create a Shortcuts Navigation Pane

You can create shortcuts to Outlook and Windows folders and files that you have saved on your computer. You can add these new shortcuts to the default Shortcuts group or create new groups.

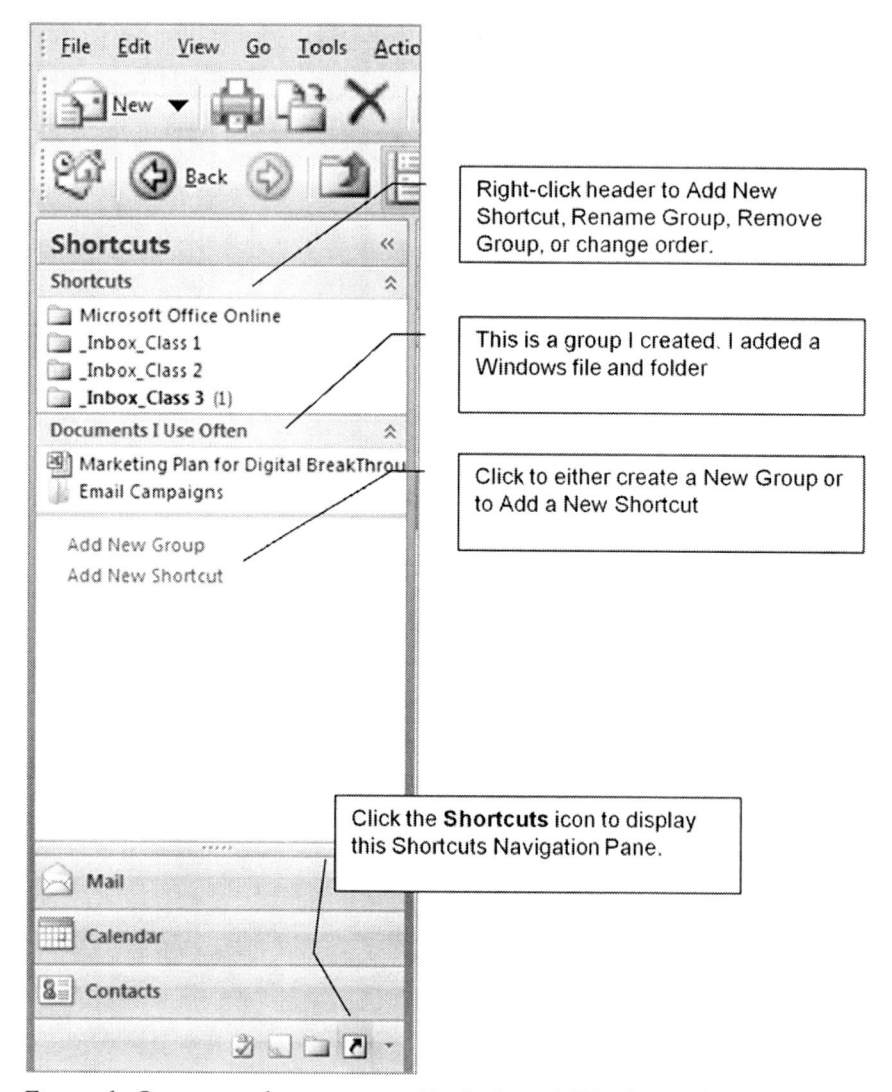

Figure 6. Create quicker access to Outlook and Windows files and folders with the Shortcuts Navigation Pane.

Add a Shortcut to an Outlook Folder

1. Click the Shortcuts icon at the bottom of the Navigation Pane to open the Shortcuts Navigation Pane (or press **Ctrl+7**).

2. Add a shortcut to the default Shortcuts group: click the **Add New Shortcut** hyperlink. Navigate to the folder you want to add, select it, and click **OK**. (I have not been able to add a shortcut to an entire Outlook folder with the included subfolders. I had to add each subfolder independently. However, adding a Windows folder that has subfolders works.)

3. Create a new group: click the **Add New Group** hyperlink, name it, and press **Enter**. Right-click the header of this new group, and click **Add New Shortcut**. Navigate to the Outlook folder you want to add, select it, and click **OK**.

Add a Shortcut to a Windows Folder

You can follow the same steps to create a shortcut to a Windows folder or file as you have for an Outlook folder with a slight adjustment. Instead of navigating to find an Outlook folder, you'll have to shrink the Outlook window so you can see it and your Windows file folders at the same time. (To open your Windows file folders, right-click the **Start** button, click **Explore**. Find the file or folder you want to add, drag it and hold it over the desired group header or Outlook folder, and drop.)

📣 *Right-click on any shortcut or group to delete it or rename it (deleting a shortcut does not delete your files). You can drag from one group to another.*

Reading Pane

Your messages will appear in full view in the Reading Pane. You can decide if you need to open them or not, and you can delete a message, preview an attachment (click on it once), and more. If you don't see the Reading Pane, click the **View** menu, point to **Reading Pane**, click **Right**.

Toolbars

Next, check to ensure you have both the Standard and Advanced toolbars displayed. Right-click anywhere on a toolbar, and click **Standard**. Repeat and click **Advanced**.

STEP 2 Create file folders for your messages instead of using your Inbox for storage. Organize your Inbox using a file structure of broad categories with like subjects together. Spend sufficient time on this now.

Create File Structure

The more organized you are, the quicker you can find what you need. From the clothes closet to your computer files, everything you touch needs to have a system. You can create subject folders for your Inbox to make retrieval of messages easier.

A basic principle of organizing is to put like items together, using broad categories with subcategories. For example, the grocery store is organized with departments that include meats, produce, breads, etc. Each department is then subcategorized (e.g., meats are separated as poultry, pork, beef, seafood). A first-level category is usually subcategorized (e.g., poultry is separated by chicken and turkey, then by parts, then by brand). This is the principle to organizing anything.

🔊 *If you want to learn more about organizing your paper and computer files so you can find answers fast, download my ebook, Get Organized At Work or purchase The Time Management Memory Jogger™ at www.PeggyDuncan.com/learnmore.htm.*

Naming Mail Folders

When you name your folders, use nouns and short, descriptive filenames. If you put a number in front of a folder name, you can make it appear in a particular order. For instance, if you keep messages coming from your clients, create a folder called "1Clients." When you add the number "1" in front of Clients, that folder will appear first (or add zeros to put a folder above that).

Separate Messages Into Folders

1. The Navigation Pane with your folder breakdown should already be displayed. If it's not, click the **View** menu, **Navigation Pane**.

2. Create all your main folders first. Right-click on the Inbox folder and click **New Folder**. Name the new folder. Repeat until all main folders have been created.

3. Create subfolders by repeating the steps, but instead of selecting the Inbox as you did when you created the main folders, you'll right-click the appropriate main folder, then create its subfolder(s).

4. Once all your folders are created, you'll file only the messages you need to keep. (Do this later. You have some more work to do that will help you clean out that mess you've let pile up.)

Create a CYA Folder

Add a **CYA** folder to your Inbox to store all messages you think you need to keep as proof that you did something, somebody said something, etc. (if you still don't know what CYA stands for, ask a buddy).

If you're in a corporate environment, you probably like to keep a lot of old email messages to CYA. Try creating a folder called CYA (or something similar), and drag all these types of messages into it.

You'll probably never need any of it, but I know it'll make you feel better having it. If you ever need to find anything in the folder, use one of Outlook's search commands to locate it (more information on finding messages begins on page 45).

You should purge this folder every three months or so, or set it up to autoarchive (see page 168).

Copy a Set of Folders

Once you have created a set of related folders, you can copy that same structure and use it for another client, event, etc.

1. Create a new folder structure in the Inbox as you normally would. Right-click the main folder (in this example Events), click **Copy "Events"**.

2. When the **Copy Folder** dialog box opens, click **Inbox** to select it (or any other desired folder), **OK**.

3. Right-click the new folder to rename it.

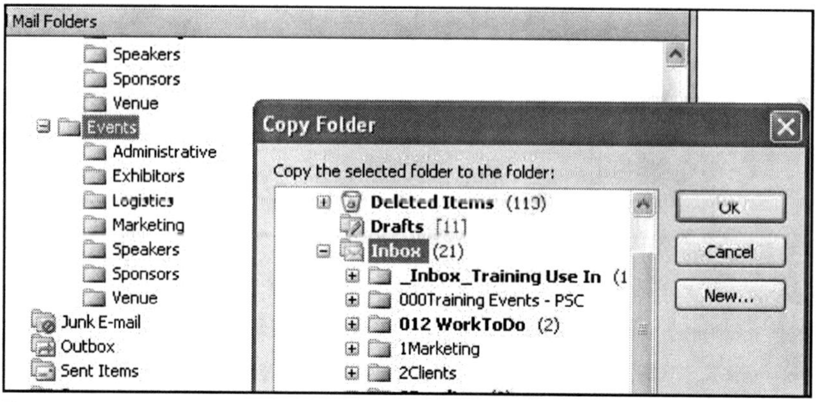

Figure 7. A second set of Events folders will be copied into the Inbox. You can right-click on the new folder to rename it.

📣 *If you need constant access to a folder or subfolder, create a shortcut to it as explained beginning on page 8.*

STEP 3
From the Inbox, change your Options to return to the Inbox "After moving or deleting an item."

Return to Inbox

After you deal with one email message, you'll want to return to the Inbox to decide what to do next (instead of having Outlook open the next message automatically).

1. Click the **Tools** menu, **Options, Email Options**.

2. Where it reads "After moving or deleting an open item:" click the drop-down box and choose **return to the Inbox**.

STEP 4 Create a default signature that will automatically display when you create new messages.

Create a Default Signature

You should create a signature line that goes out with each email message. Use it to explain who you are and how to contact you other than by email. If you're a business owner, why not add a line about what you do and a live link to your Web site?

Some people have a personal signature and another for business. It's simpler for me to use one for all messages.

1. Click the **Tools** menu, **Options**, **Mail Format** tab.

2. Click the **Signatures** button near the bottom of the dialog box, click **New,** name the signature, **OK**.

3. Type desired signature in the blank text box. Add all your contact information, spacing paragraphs and line breaks as you normally would (as in addressing a letter, **Shift+Enter** to create line breaks instead of inserting paragraphs by pressing Enter. This will prevent double spaces).

   Change the font, click to include your business card if desired, and add your logo by clicking the **Insert Picture** button. You can also add hyperlinks to Web sites by clicking the **Hyperlink** button.

4. Consider adding a message that will limit the junk from people you know: "Please do not add my name to your distribution list for jokes, prayers, thoughts for the day, chain letters, etc. Thanks!"

5. Click **OK** until you're back out.

📣 *I don't recommend adding graphics to your signature because they appear as attachments in some email clients and Webmail.*

PEACE.

Peggy Duncan, Personal Productivity Expert
PSC Press – 404-492-8197 Atlanta
worksmart@PeggyDuncan.com
http://www.PeggyDuncan.com

My Workshops
Find Time to Lead
Get Organized So You Can Think!
Spend Less Time Working but Get More Done
Computer Magic!
Marketing Collateral Using PowerPoint
Manage Time with Outlook
PowerPoint - Advanced
PowerPoint All the Way
Shameless Self-Promotion: DIY SEO

....
Please do not add my name to your distribution list
for jokes, prayers, thoughts for the day, or
chain letters. Thanks.

Figure 8. This is a sample of the main signature I use with each message. I don't recommend adding graphics to your signature because they appear as attachments in some email clients and Webmail.

Create Different Signatures for Each Email Account

If you've set up various email accounts, you can create different signatures to use with them (e.g., you may want the signature on a personal account to be more casual than your business email signature, or perhaps you have several businesses and want to use a different signature for each one).

Once you've created the different signatures, you can connect each email account with the appropriate one.

1. Click the **Tools** menu, **Options**, **Mail Format** tab, **Signatures**.

2. Under **Choose default signature**, choose the email account you want to change. Under **New messages**, choose the signature you want to use for that email account. If you want a different signature for **Replies/forwards**, do it here.

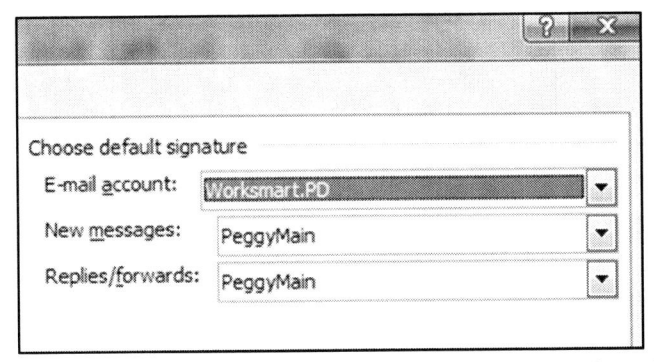

Figure 9. Choose your default signature to use with each email account if you need to.

After you have this set up, you can choose which email account to send a message from. The matching signature for that account is now already in place. Create a new message as you normally would. If you want to use any email account other than the default, click **Account**, and choose.

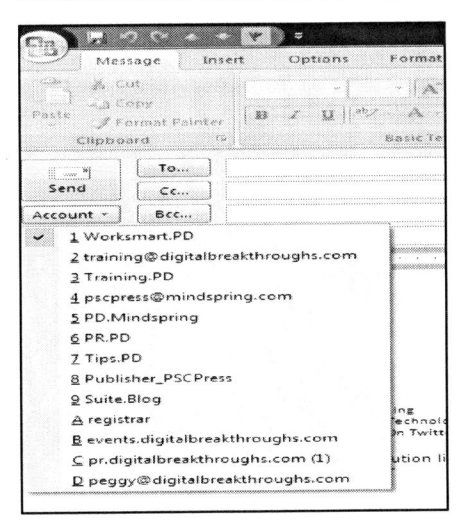

Figure 10. Choose from your various email accounts when you create a message.

Switch Signatures Inside a Message

You can switch signatures in a new message by right-clicking on the signature and choosing a different one. New to Outlook 2007, you can only insert one signature at a time.

STEP 5
Create email responses you use all the time (such as directions to your office) and save for easier access.

Create Repetitive Responses

You may have to send someone the same information often, as in directions to your office. You can save the information as an entry in Quick Parts, a signature, a message filed away, or a template.

Quick Parts

Quick Parts is new to Outlook 2007 and is described as a gallery of "building blocks" that allows you to save and reuse text and images. These building blocks are saved to the default email template file called NormalEmail.dotm.

1. Select text or an image such as directions to your office or your company logo. From a new or open message, click the **Insert** tab. In the Text group, click **Quick Parts** (if it's grayed out, click in the body of the message), **Save Selection to Quick Parts Gallery**.

2. Give your entry a meaningful and short name, choose or create a category (good idea to create broad categories because Outlook sorts them by category first, then by name), write a description, choose where to save it and how it should be inserted, **OK**.

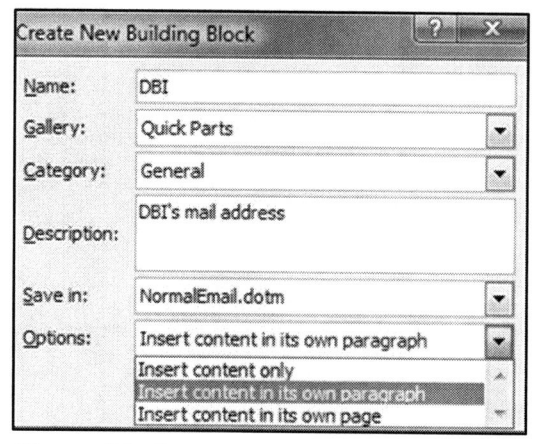

Figure 11. Save text or images you use often in the Quick Parts Gallery. You can insert them in Contacts, Calendar, and Tasks.

To use the entry later, click inside the body of the message where you want it to go, click the **Insert** tab, **Quick Parts,** and click your choice. (Or you can type the name of the entry and press F3). In the Quick Parts window, when you see the information you want to insert on a page, you can right-click on it for more placement options.

To change the options in Figure 11, click **Quick Parts,** right-click on the building block you want to change, **Edit Properties,** and make your changes.

To change the text or graphic in a building block, display it on a page, make your changes, follow the steps to create it (giving it the same name), and click **Yes** to redefine the entry.

To delete an entry, click **Quick Parts,** right-click on any entry, **Organize and Delete,** make your choice, and click **Delete.**

📣 *I added Quick Parts to my Quick Access Toolbar for easier access. Refer to page 20 for instructions in Word that work the same in Outlook. It's also a good idea to keep Quick Parts backed up (see page 171).*

Use Signatures for Responses

When you created your signature that goes out at the bottom of each message you send (on page 13), that text could be anything. In previous versions of Outlook, I'd created signatures for all kinds of information that I sent often. However, in Outlook 2007, you can only insert one signature at a time, so I've transferred these other signatures to Quick Parts.

Create the Message and Save as msg

You may need to save a message outside of Outlook. You can create a message as you normally would, add the subject line, the body, any attachments, and a signature. Then you'll save it somewhere convenient in the .msg file format. Anytime you need it, open it, address the message, and send as you normally would (find instructions on page 62).

Create a Template for Your Message

You can also create a template or shell of a message and customize it.

1. Create a new message as you normally would, customizing it with names on the To, Bcc, and/or Cc lines, a subject, content with formatting, and attachments.

2. Save the email as a template. Click the **Office** button, point to **Save As**, and click **Save As**.

3. In the Save as type drop-down list (under the File name box), choose **Outlook Template (*.oft)**.

4. Give the template a meaningful name and choose a file location (I usually accept the default folder of Templates, and have a new folder designated for Outlook templates).

5. Click **Save & Close** the message you'd created.

Later, when you want to send an email based on the template:

1. Click the **Tools** menu, **Forms**, **Choose Form**.

2. From the Look In drop-down list, choose **User Templates in File System**, double-click your template to open a copy.

3. Make any necessary changes and send as you normally would (original template remains intact).

📢 *If you decide to use templates, add a shortcut to Choose Form to the Quick Access Toolbar (see instructions beginning on page 20).*

Delete a Template

If you ever decide to delete a template, you'll have to find it on your computer.

1. Follow Steps 1 and 2 in the previous instructions (but don't click to open the template). Copy the path to the file to your Clipboard.

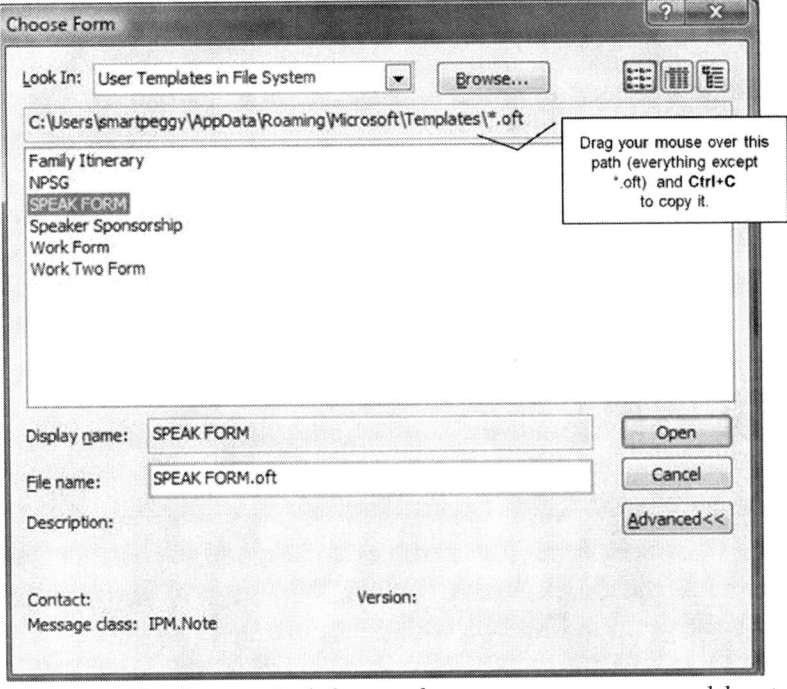

Figure 12. You have to find the template on your computer to delete it.

2. Next, you'll go to this location on your computer. Click the Windows **Start** button, **Explore**. Click on the folder that appears in the Address Bar, **Ctrl+V** (shortcut to paste) to replace text with the path you copied, and press **Enter**. Delete the template.

Figure 13. Paste the path to your templates in the Address Bar.

Create an Autoresponder

If you have information that you send often, you could set up a special email address with an autoresponder that sends it out. For example, you are head of

|19

community affairs and people are always contacting you about how to apply for funds to help their non-profit. You'll have a special email address called "funding@yourcompany.com." That email address is on a special business card you use at networking events. It's also on your Web site.

When someone sends an email message to that address, your automated response tells them all they need to know, including links to pages on your Web site, etc.

📢 *The autoresponder should also include your regular email address in case the recipient has additional questions. Don't misuse or overuse autoresponders!*

STEP 6 Customize Word's Quick Access Toolbar.

Customize Word's Quick Access Toolbar

Email a document from Word with one click: add the FileSendAsAttachment command to the Quick Access Toolbar. When you click this command, a new message will open in Outlook with your document attached.

1. Open Word, click the **Customize Quick Access Toolbar** button, and click **More Commands.**

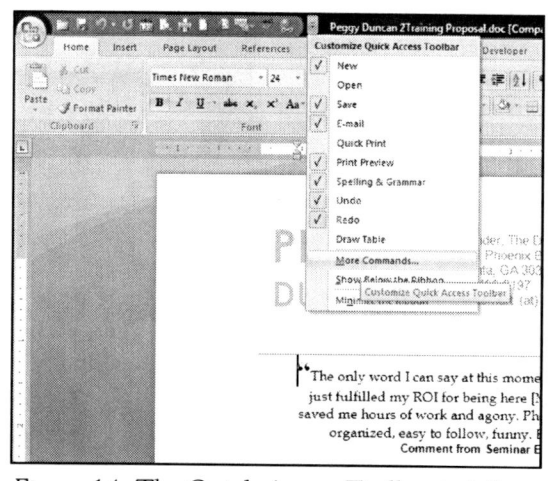

Figure 14. The Quick Access Toolbar is fully customizable.

2. On the left, *Word Options side*, **Customize** should be highlighted. On the right side under *Choose commands from*, choose **All Commands**.

3. Scroll to find the **Email (FileSendAsAttachment)** command. Double-click the command to move to the right side, click **OK**. Click it when you need it.

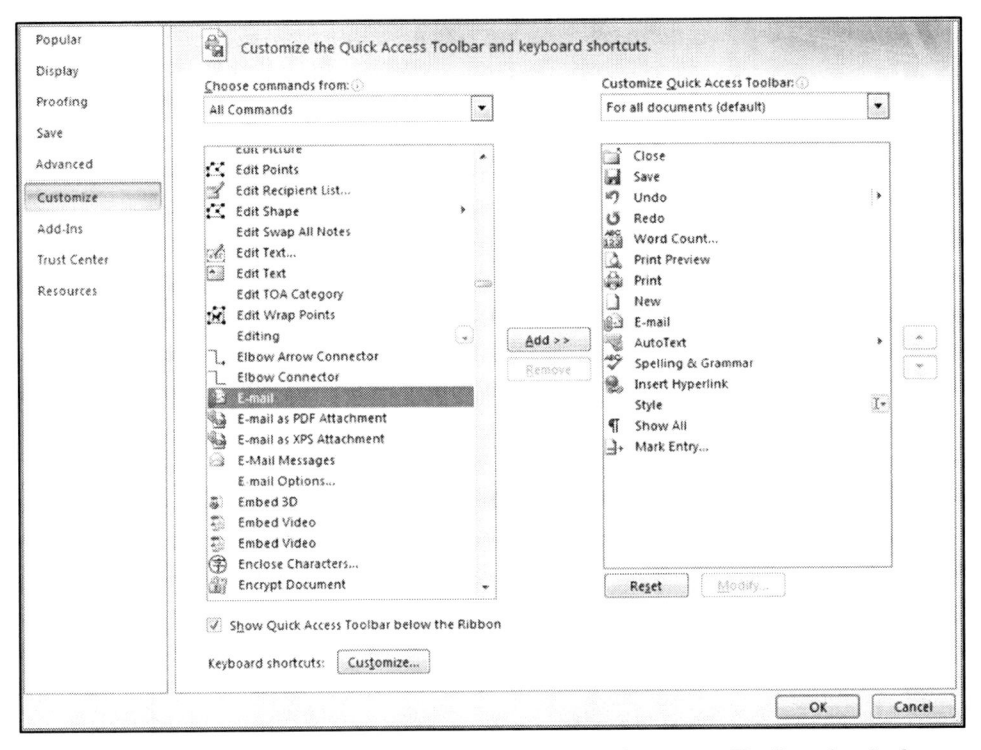

Figure 15. You can add any command to the Quick Access Toolbar by finding it here and clicking **Add**. *You can also create a keyboard shortcut here.*

To rearrange the order of how these commands appear on the Quick Access Toolbar, click the up/down buttons on the far right. You can also choose whether to customize the toolbar for all documents or only for the one you're working in (see box next to All Commands).

|21

STEP 7 Put your best face forward by turning on Spelling Check (if you think you need it).

Turn On Spelling Check

Spelling Check. You may want to run Spelling Check on messages before sending. In the main Outlook window, click the **Tools** menu, **Options**, **Spelling** tab. Tick **Always check spelling before sending** box.

On the other hand, if you decide to check your spelling on individual messages, click the **ABC Spelling** command inside each message.

Custom Dictionary

Once you turn on Spelling Check, you may want to add your industry or company jargon to the dictionary so your software will recognize certain words, acronyms, etc., and not mark them as errors. In the same dialog box as the previous tip, click **Spelling and AutoCorrection**, **Custom Dictionaries**, **Edit Word List**, and type the word or phrase you want to add, pressing **Enter** after each.

Sync Other Email Accounts to Outlook

If you have other email accounts with various providers such as Hotmail, MSN, etc., save time checking your messages by finding out how to sync all of it with Outlook (check their Web site).

You'll be able to check all messages at once, right from Outlook, without needing to visit a company's Web site, get distracted by ads and entertainment news, and waste more time.

EMAIL - MANAGE MESSAGES

How many messages are in your Inbox right now? Hundreds? Thousands? They represent unfinished work, demands on your time, missed deadlines, broken promises, and a whole lot of junk. They frustrate you every time you have to scroll through them, but you go day in and day out letting them pile up, with no end in sight.

When you scroll through screens and screens of messages, you're cramming your brain with split-second thoughts such as "call Joe, forgot the meeting, what does she need?, oops, I forgot about that, huh?, call Steve, don't have time to do this, report is due, what the heck is this?, customer needs help, I need help, *#!!?...." On the other hand, with a clean, organized Inbox, you'll do something with each message and put controls in place to remember what needs to be done and when.

Change How You Use the Inbox

Your Inbox is packed with hundreds or thousands of messages because you're using it for storage. The Inbox is for active messages and is not a long-term storage solution. The Inbox is **not** a:

- To do list for unfinished work.
- Tickler file that reminds you of work.
- Calendar with meeting notices and reminders.
- Database for addresses and phone numbers.
- Filing system for unfinished projects.

Use your Inbox for a few active messages only!

Once you sit down to check your messages, consider yourself in a meeting with your Inbox, and deal with each one. Just as you do with paper, touch the message, and do something with it: either do it, delete, schedule, forward, file, flag, or delegate it. Printing adds to the mess so don't do it unless you absolutely have to.

You may not be able to control how many messages people send you. But you sure can manage what happens to them once they land in your Inbox.

YOUR GOAL: To always see the bottom of your Inbox without scrolling!

Best Time to Check Email

There are several schools of thought about when to check email. Some consultants suggest not checking it in the morning because you'll get distracted, look up, and your day is shot. Others say check it three times a day: once in the morning, right before lunch, and once before you leave work. Still others will tell you to check email once a day.

You're going to have to create a routine that works best for you. When I'm working on something important and need to stay focused, I close Outlook and take breaks to check email. (When Outlook is closed, I use my cell phone or PDA to remind me of meetings, etc.) When I'm working on something I can do in my sleep and I'm ahead of schedule, I'll check email as I'm working.

Just about everything that happens for me begins with email. I'm rarely a day away from it, and I don't want to be. I work with busy people who want answers fast, and because I'm organized, keep my Inbox to one screen, and use every advantage Outlook offers, I'm able to handle most things quickly.

Establish a Routine

You do not have to be available the instant a new email message arrives. If it's that critical, I'm sure they would have called. Consider establishing a routine for checking email that best fits your schedule. Experiment with how often you need to check it until you find the right fit for you.

Email Addict

If you're hooked on email and find yourself checking it even when you're working on something important and need to stay focused, you're going to have to break the habit. These simple changes could help.

- **Don't start Outlook when your computer starts.** Right-click on the **Start** menu, click **Explore**, find your **Startup** folder, and move Outlook out of it.

- Turn off the New Message Alert that appears every time you receive a new message (see page 56 for instructions).

- Deactivate the new message sound alert and "the ding" (see page 57 for instructions).

- Make the default view in Outlook the Calendar (or Tasks). Click the **Tools** menu, **Options**, **Other** tab, **Advanced Options**, **Browse**, click **Calendar** (or Tasks).

- Turn off the option of automatically checking for incoming messages. Click the **Tools** menu, **Options**, **Mail Setup** tab, **Send/Receive**, untick **Schedule an automatic send/receive**, OK. When you need to check email, click the **Send/Receive** toolbar button.

- **Make it inconvenient to open Outlook.** Remove Outlook from the System Tray (to the right of the Start button). Right-click on the **Outlook** icon, and click **Delete** (this does not delete the software).

Next, remove Outlook from the Start menu. Click the **Start** button. If the **Outlook** icon is there, right-click on it, and click **Remove from this list**.

To open Outlook later, you'll have to find it. Click **Start**, point to **All Programs**, point to **Microsoft Office**, click **Outlook**.

- **Work on one computer and use another one for email.** This will be an inconvenience, but try it until you kick the email habit.

Going forward, every time you realize you've stopped working on a project and jumped back to email, stop. Remove your hands from the keyboard, take a deep breath, then retrace your steps. Back up to what you were doing before you checked email. Do this each time, and you'll start to change.

It'll take you approximately 21 days to break the habit, so don't give up. Email news is rarely earth-shattering. If someone needs you badly enough, she should pick up the phone or walk two doors down to see if you're busy. Start now and do everything you can to break the hold email has on you.

Methods for Clearing the Inbox

You have to learn how to prioritize your messages and distinguish between something that needs your immediate attention, what can wait, and what deserves none of your time.

- **Relevant, important, and urgent.** This is something that needs to be done right now.

- **Relevant, important, but not urgent.** This is work you'll need to do but not right away (unless it's quick and you can handle it in less than one minute).

- **For information only.** You're Cc'd on something because the sender was too lazy to discern who actually needed it. Or it's information that's part of an ongoing discussion and you may or may not need the details. Or how about all those RSS feeds you subscribe to but rarely get a chance to read? This type of email does not require you to take action so it's a lower priority.

- **Noise.** A bunch of legitimate emails that contribute much to your information overload but little to your goals. This includes social media rants (some of this is good, of course), office gossip, jokes from friends, and so on.

- **Junk or spam.** With excellent security features built into Outlook, you shouldn't be bothered a lot by spam. If you are, see information on junk email beginning on page 27.

To help you get to one screen and manage what you need to do with ease, the mess that's in your Inbox and the new messages coming in will be dealt with using the following five methods.

- ☒ Eliminate junk email so you're only managing legitimate mail.
- ☒ Redirect messages with rules based on content, origin, and importance.
- ☒ Categorize messages and view them in batches with one click.
- ☒ Remember to do the work using flags, Tasks, and the Calendar.
- ☒ File the keepers.

First Method: Eliminate Junk Email

The first step toward clearing the Inbox is dealing with spam. Spam comprises as much as 75 percent of online messages, and according to the Federal Trade Commission, about two-thirds of it involves some type of fraud. At this writing, legislation will do nothing to curb spam, but with Outlook's built-in filters and other software on the market, you can control it.

When you receive unsolicited email that is clearly junk, don't respond. Responding only verifies to the sender that yours is a valid email address. Instead, add them to your Blocked Senders List and delete the message without opening it. The Blocked Senders List will block any future email coming from that email address. This could help with some email, but professional spammers change their email addresses automatically. Spam-blocking technology is your best option.

One of the best ways to fight spam is to avoid putting your clickable email address on the Web. Spammers use software (spambots) to find the @ symbol (including inside a PDF), and they harvest the addresses. (I write my address as follows: worksmart at PeggyDuncan.com, using uneven spacing. People contacting me are smart enough to know what to do from there.

📣 *It's not a good idea to use email addresses that are too common such as info@ or sales@. Spammers take any domain and automatically add these addresses to their lists.*

Change How Junk Email Gets Filtered

Outlook's junk email filter is based on four levels of protection. You can set Outlook's filters to **High** and most all junk email will be detected and sent to the Junk E-mail folder (located in the Navigation Pane).

1. From within the Inbox, click the **Actions** menu, point to **Junk Email**, click **Junk E-mail Options** (or right-click on any message in your Inbox, point to Junk E-mail, click Junk E-mail Options).

2. Click the **Options** tab. Tick your choice. I have mine set at High, and I check the JunkE-mail folder first to make sure legitimate messages haven't landed there.

Move Messages from Junk E-mail Folder

In the list of Junk E-mail Options mentioned previously, you'll see a command that allows you to permanently delete suspected junk email as opposed to sending it to the Junk E-mail folder. Do not tick this option in case legitimate messages get misdirected.

Regardless of the controls you put in place, a few junk messages will still get through and legitimate messages will land in the Junk E-mail folder. When that happens, make the following change.

1. Click the **Junk E-mail** folder to view its contents.

2. Move legitimate messages to your Inbox (right-click on each one, point to **Junk E-Mail**, and click **Mark as Not Junk**).

3. You'll be prompted to add the sender or mailing list name to your **Safe Senders** or **Safe Recipients List**.

If you find that you still need more protection, there are lots of options available, from free to annual subscriptions. Following is a partial list of spam sites and software.

Web Sites

www.SPAMhelp.org

www.zdnet.com (read reviews on different software)

Software

Cloudmark Desktop is a powerful spam fighter. It's the only product that I personally recommend. The technology is subscription-based. It also spots fake email messages that ask you to give up all your personal bank account information (called phishing). Visit www.cloudmark.com.

Empty Junk E-mail Folder

1. Right-click on the **Junk E-mail** folder (located in the Navigation Pane).

2. Hold down the **Shift** key and click **Empty "Junk E-mail" Folder**. Holding down the Shift key deletes the messages from your computer. Otherwise, they would go into the Deleted Items folder and you'll have to delete them again.

Add to Blocked Senders List

When junk email gets past the filters and lands in your Inbox, add the sender to your Blocked Senders List.

1. From the Inbox, right-click on the unopened message, point to **Junk E-mail**.

2. Click **Add Sender to Blocked Senders List** (this is also where you add people to your Safe Senders List).

📢 *You're wasting your time doing this if you don't put the controls I've mentioned in place. You'll get too much spam for the professionals, and you won't be able to keep up.*

Oops! Delete from Blocked Senders List

At some point, you may add someone to your Blocked Senders List by mistake.

1. Click once on the **Junk E-mail** folder in the Navigation Pane to view its contents.
2. Right-click on the message you need to move, point to **Junk E-mail**, click **Mark as Not Junk** (or select the message and press Ctrl+Alt+J).

The following is another way to remove addresses from the Blocked Senders List.

1. From the Inbox, click the **Actions** menu, point to **Junk Email**, click **Junk E-mail Options** (or right-click the message).
2. Click the **Blocked Senders** tab. Once inside the Blocked Senders List, type the first letter of the email address you're looking for and scroll until you find it.
3. Click on the name you added by mistake, click **Remove, OK**.

Use Signature Line to Discourage Junk

If you're on the receiving end of useless messages such as jokes, thoughts for the day, or chain letters, put your signature to work and let people know you do not appreciate it. Create an automatic signature (see instructions on page 13) that will go out with every message you send and add this:

"Please do not add my name to your distribution list for jokes, prayers, thoughts for the day, chain letters, etc. Thanks!"

Ask People You Know to Stop Sending Junk

When you receive unwanted messages from people you know, ask them to stop. (If a spiel similar to the following doesn't work, call them and tell them to stop. Be firm.)

"I appreciate your thinking about me, but in an effort to streamline my email messages and manage my time, I have to ask you to remove my name from the distribution list you're using. Thanks!"

Add to Safe Senders List

Just as you can add people to the Blocked Senders List, you can also add to the Safe Senders List (use the same instructions as you used to Add to Blocked Senders List but choose Safe Senders, page 29).

- By default, the check box to include everyone in your Contacts folder is ticked.
- If you want people who you correspond with (but are not in your **Contacts**) to be considered safe senders, tick **Automatically add people I e-mail to the Safe Senders List**.
- If Automatic Picture Download is turned off, messages from or to email addresses (or domain names) on the **Safe Senders** and **Safe Recipients** lists will be treated as exceptions and the blocked content will be downloaded.

If a message automatically goes to the Junk E-mail folder by mistake, go to the Junk E-mail folder, right-click on the message, and click **Add Sender to Safe Senders List** or **Add Recipient to Safe Recipients List** (choose this latter option if the email is addressed to a list and your name isn't on the To line).

If you want the message sent to your Inbox, right-click on it, and press **Ctrl+Alt+J** (the shortcut for Mark as Not Junk).

You can also type a list of names or domains to add to the list.

1. From within the Inbox, click the **Actions** menu, point to **Junk E-mail**, click **Junk E-mail Options, Safe Senders** tab, **Add**.
2. To add an email address, type it as you normally would. To add a domain, type the domain (without www), click **OK** (or press Enter).

The domain will appear with the @ symbol when it's added.

Create a Disposable Email Address

If you leave your email address in a chat room, with Newsgroups, etc., it will be harvested by spammers 100 percent of the time. Instead of using one of your actual addresses, you can generate a disposable email address that points email sent to it to your real address. The disposable email address will self-destruct after a certain period of time that you set. (If you shop on the Web, temporary email addresses could be a perfect solution instead of entering your main one.)

Following are some Web sites with more information.

www. emailias.com   www.spamex.com

www.mailinator.com   www.spamgourmet.com

📢 *You could also set up regular email accounts in Outlook and create and delete them as needed, but you may have to wait a couple of days for your service provider to activate the new address.*

Cloak Your Email Address on the Web

If you put an email address on the Web, spambots that cruise the Web looking for the @ symbol will harvest it. There is no valid reason to put your full email address on the Web. Simply type it without the @ symbol (e.g., worksmart at peggyduncan.com or worksmart a/(t) PeggyDuncan.com). The same applies to any PDFs you upload.

Second Method: Redirect Messages with Rules

Now that you've stopped the spam, it's important to continue examining the types of messages you're getting. If you're receiving newsletters that you rarely read, click to unsubscribe. Too many messages from public forums? Opt for a daily digest or get out now. Family and friends sending you jokes you like but don't have time for? Redirect them to a folder and read at your leisure. Receiving a lot of messages because everyone copies everything to everybody? Change your corporate email culture and make this stop.

Next, you'll move to the second step and set up rules to redirect messages to other folders, including Deleted Items. You can also create rules that will make certain messages stand out.

Color-Code Messages from Certain Senders

You can create a rule to have messages from certain senders automatically change color.

1. From inside the Inbox, click once on a message from anyone for which you'd like to set up this rule.

2. Click the **Tools** menu, **Organize**.

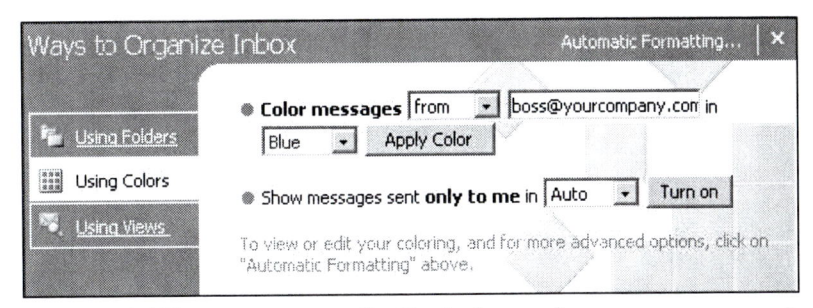

Figure 16. This instruction tells Outlook to color any message coming from this email address Blue as it enters the Inbox.

3. Select the **Using Colors** option and choose the desired color.
4. Click the **x** to close.

Send Messages to Special Folder

You can create a rule to automatically move a message from a certain sender into a particular folder (e.g., your boss or administrative assistant, especially when the message is addressed only to you).

1. From the Mail folder (Inbox view), click the **Tools** menu, click **Rules and Alerts**, **New Rule**.

2. In Step 1-Stay Organized, click **Move messages from someone to a folder**. To create a simple rule, use a rules template. For more complex rules, start with a blank one. (Always read the text in the dialog box: it guides you through the Wizard to set up your rules.)

3. Down in Step 2, you'll edit the rule description. Click **people or distribution list**, find desired person, and double-click the name to place it in the From box, **OK**.

4. Continuing with the rule description, click **specified,** and choose the folder to send the message to. (If you need to create the folder, click New, create the new folder, select it, click OK.)

5. Once you've selected the appropriate folder, click **Next** to have this rule apply to all messages. Or to limit the messages that the rule

applies to, in the **Which condition(s) do you want to check** list, tick any options you want.

6. Click **Next**. In this step, tick any additional conditions you may want to apply.

7. Click **Next**. Now tick any exceptions that will apply to this rule (if any).

8. Give your new rule a name, then tick to **Run this rule now on messages in "Inbox"** and **Finish**.

From now on, messages coming into your Inbox from this email address will automatically go to the folder you chose. You may want to take time now to create a rule to send messages from your boss or your assistant to special folders. These will be the mail folders you check first. Don't go overboard with this rule.

📣 *Also consider creating a rule that sends messages you're CC'd on to a Read folder to review later. You'll have to create the rule for each of your email addresses.*

Move Messages With Certain Subject Line

You can create a rule that sends messages with a certain subject line into a designated folder. For example, you send an email with "RSVP: Upcoming Outlook Workshop" in the subject line. When you receive the replies, all messages with this subject line go into a special folder you've already created.

Refer to the previous lesson. The steps to create this rule are very similar, except in Step 2, you'll choose to **Move messages with specific words in the subject line to a folder**. And in Step 3, you'll edit the rule description by clicking **specific words**.

Change a Rule

Once you create a rule, you can change it by clicking the **Tools** menu, **Rules and Alerts**. Click the rule you want to change, and click the **Change Rule** button. Choose to either **Edit Rule Settings** or **Rename Rule**, and make desired changes.

Third Method: Separate Inbox Messages with Categories

Now it's time to prioritize email with categories and groups based on certain criteria. Categories can have custom names, designated colors, and custom shortcut keys.

You can use Outlook's default categories or create and customize your own. The following is an example of a category I use to separate email messages requesting my services to speak at an event.

Category – 1RequestToSpeak

I'm always receiving messages from meeting planners or companies inquiring about my availability and fees to speak at an event. I created a category called "1RequestToSpeak." I also created a search folder and can view these items later with the click of a button. (I put the "1" in front of my category name so it would show at the top of the list.)

When the message arrives:

- If I'm looking at the message in the Inbox, I'll either:
    o Click the blank category box to the right of the message, or
    o Click the **Categorize** button, or
    o Right-click the message, point to **Categorize**, click **1RequestToSpeak**, or
    o Drag the message down to this category in my Inbox.

Whenever you don't see the category you need when you click Categorize, click **All Categories**

- If the message is open, I'll click the **Categorize** command in the Options group on the Ribbon.

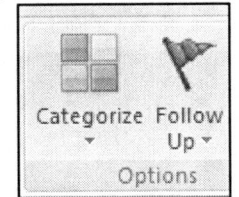

Before you start creating categories, think them through first (e.g., projects you work on, important inquiries you receive, etc.) The following categories represent my most important email messages that I'll handle first.

- **0Urgent.** This is important and urgent. I need to do this right away or sometime today. By assigning the category, I can keep messages prioritized. When the work is something I can do quickly, I'll do it. Otherwise, I'll schedule time on my calendar to get it done.

- **1RequestToSpeak.** Someone's sent an inquiry asking me to speak at their convention or company.

- **3CALL.** Someone has emailed me and I'll need to call them at some point. I'll also flag this message for follow up.

- **4MEET.** Someone wants to meet with me. This type of email is usually settled pretty quickly after a couple of responses or a phone call, so I leave it in my Inbox and deal with it. Once the meeting is set and that information is on my calendar, I'll insert the message into my calendar as an item and delete the message.

- **5Registered.** Someone has registered for a workshop or Webinar at www.DigitalBreakThroughs.com. Payment for training comes in via PayPal and has certain words in the subject line, body, and only comes to one email account. Because every email arrives with very specific and consistent words, a rule adds the category and then sends it to a special folder.

- **6PROSPECT.** Potential coaching or consulting client has contacted me. I don't have a rule to move this type of email to a folder because there are too many variables. However, by assigning the category, I can keep similar messages together. These are all filed in the same Mail folder. If I think it's a serious prospect, I'll flag it for follow up.

These categorized messages can be filtered and displayed quickly in the Inbox by clicking the Categories header. They will line up either at the bottom or top of the Inbox (click the header until it's where you prefer. I sometimes go back and forth).

I've also created a search folder for some of these types of messages and can view them by category regardless of where they're filed.

🔊 *You'll learn all about these options throughout this chapter.*

Create a Category

Here's how to create a category (after you've thought them through…don't just start creating them). You can rename the default categories and also create more from scratch.

1. From the Inbox, click the **Edit** menu, **Categorize, New** (or click the Categorize Button, **All Categories, New**) .

2. Give the category a meaningful name, designate a color, choose a keyboard shortcut key (optional), **OK**.

Assign a Category

Once your categories are created, it's easy to assign one or more to a message. Select the message, click the **Categorize** button, and click the one you want (you can repeat and add more). If you don't see the category you want, scroll down to the end of the list, click **All Categories**.

In the Inbox, you'll see the color box in the Categories column next to the message. Inside the message, the category is indicated by a color bar just under the Ribbon.

Another way to add a category is to drag the message down from the Inbox to the Categories pane, releasing it under the appropriate category.

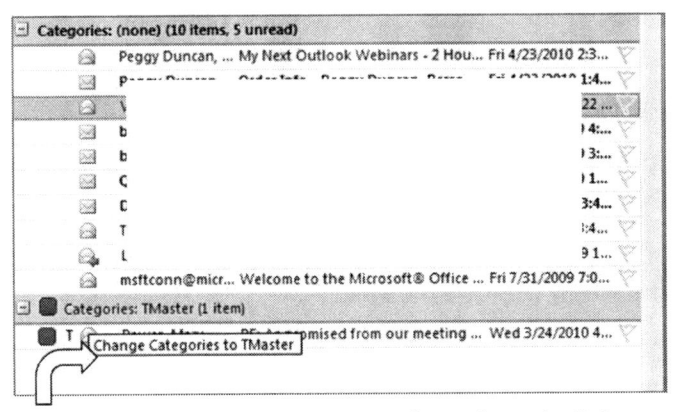

Figure 17. You can drag a message down from the Inbox to Categories.

Set Quick Click

You can create a shortcut to the category you use most with Set Quick Click. (This feature turned out to be more trouble than it was worth so I stopped using it. See my note.)

1. Right-click any category color box and click **Set Quick Click**.
2. Choose the desired category, **OK**.

Once it's set, use it by clicking the empty color box in the Categories column of your Inbox.

📢 You'll have to be careful with this. When you set it up, it works across the rest of Outlook. And anytime you left-click in a Categories column, the category you set up as Quick Click will be assigned. If you make this mistake, right-click and **Clear All Categories**. This few seconds this command saved me wasn't worth the frustration it caused every time I clicked by mistake. To stop using it, click the **Categorize** button, **Set Quick Click**, choose **no category**. (However, I'm OK using this feature for flags.)

Change a Category

You can change an assigned category. The least confusing way to do this is to open the item, right-click the category bar that lists the category name, and click to delete it.

Remove a Category

To remove a category from a message, right-click the color box next to it, **Categorize, Clear All Categories**.

Create a Rule for a Category

You can create a rule that automatically adds the category to a message and then moves it to a folder.

1. Click the **Tools** menu, **Rules and Alerts, New Rule, Check messages when they arrive, Next**.
2. In Step 1, I ticked the following boxes: **with specific words in the subject, through a specified account, with specific words in the body, and assigned to category**.

3. In Step 2, I clicked **specified account** and chose *pscpress@mindspring.com*. I clicked **specific words** (in the subject line), and typed *Payment received from*, **Add, OK**. I clicked **specific words in the body** and typed *Hello PSC Press*. Then I clicked **category** and chose the *5Registered* category.

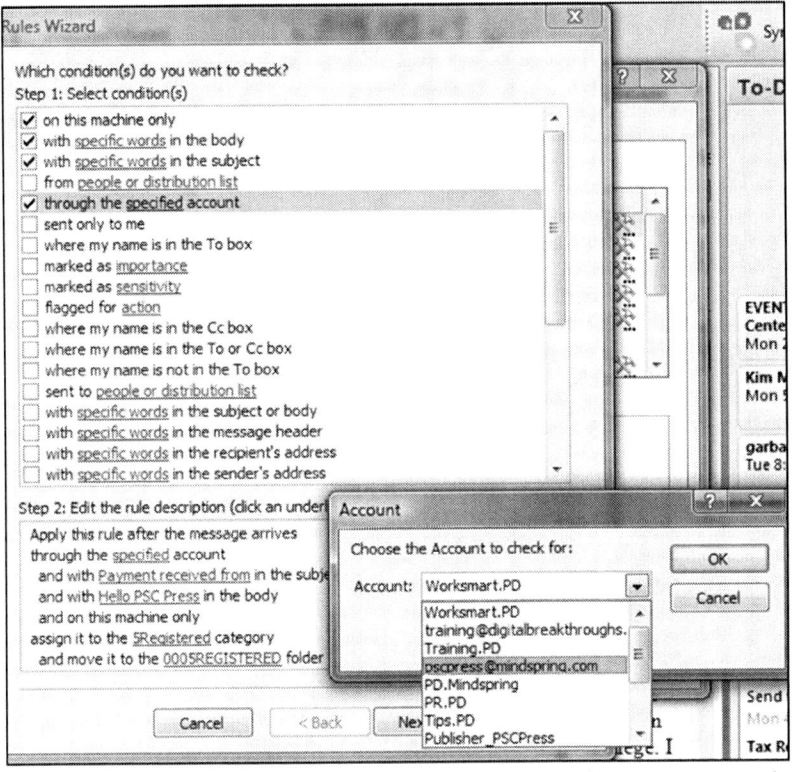

Figure 18. Always look at Step 1 and Step 2 on each screen to see what needs to be changed.

4. On the next screen, in Step 1, I ticked the **move it to the specified folder** box.

5. In Step 2, I clicked **specified** and chose the *0005Registered* folder in the Inbox. Then **Next, Next,** named the rule, **Finish**.

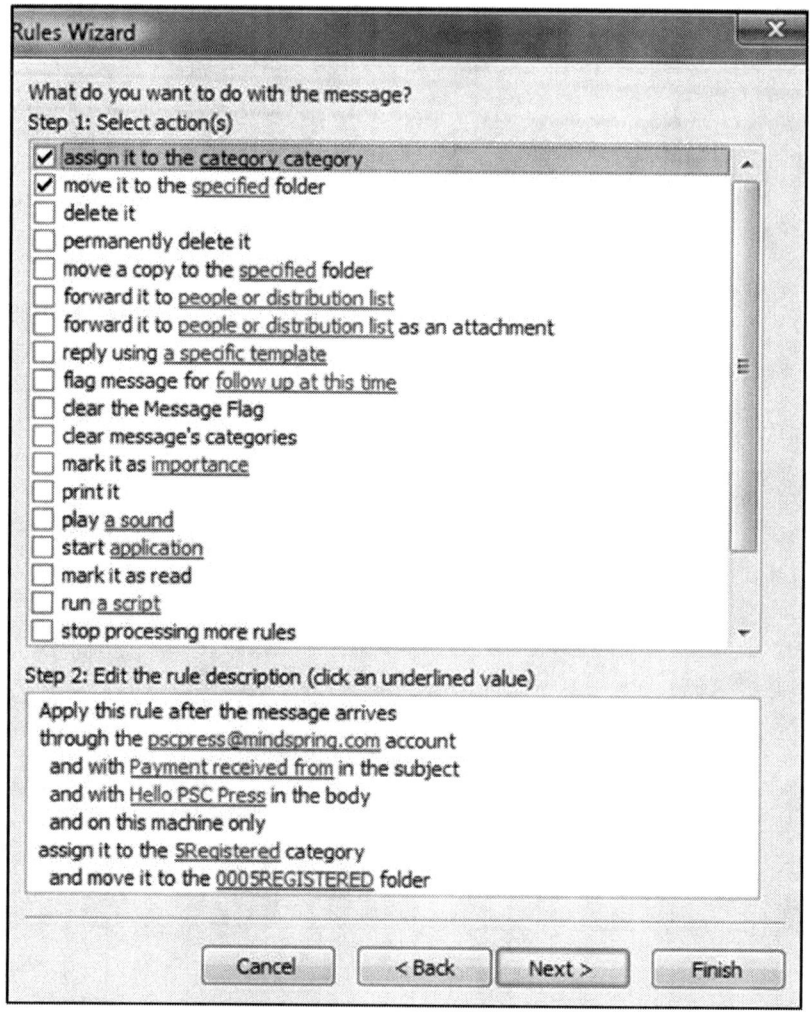

Figure 19. Continue to follow Step 1 and Step 2 on each screen to see what needs to be changed.

Fourth Method: Flag Messages for Follow-Up

With so many things going on, let Outlook flags help you remember. You can flag incoming and outgoing messages, and you can flag messages in any folder, including the Sent Items folder.

Once flagged, a copy of the message will appear in the For Follow Up Search Folder (more information on Search Folders begins on page 49), the To-Do Bar, and Tasks. To open the flagged message anywhere, double-click it.

📣 CAUTION: *If you delete a flagged message from your Inbox (or folder), it's deleted everywhere. If you want the option of hiding the message in your Inbox and keeping it as a task, change how you view your Inbox and hide flagged messages (see page 44). Or drag the message to Tasks and create an item there (more on Tasks in the next chapter).*

Flag Without a Reminder

You can flag a message with or without a specific reminder date to do the work. Right-click the flag icon (to the right of the message), and click one of the defaults.

📣 *A copy of the flagged message will land on the To-Do Bar. At times, you may want to change the message's subject line on the To-Do Bar so you'll know at a glance what you need to do. The subject line in the email message will remain unchanged.*

Flag With a Reminder

If you want to remember to do the work at a specific time, you can add a reminder to the flagged item.

1. Right-click on the flag to the right of the message (in the Flag column) and click **Add Reminder** (or select the message and **Ctrl+Shift+G**).

2. Click the **Flag to** drop-down box and choose the type of reminder you need (or you can type any words you want here (see Figure 20 on page 43).

3. Set the **Start date** and **Due by** using the drop-down calendar or by typing words such as "next Wednesday."

4. Set a **Reminder** date and time, **OK**.

📢 *If you don't do the work on the date you set, it'll automatically move to the next day.*

Set Quick Click for Reminders

You can set up a default time frame for flag reminders.

1. Right-click the flag icon located at the right of a message (Flags column), point to **Follow Up**, and click **Set Quick Click**.

2. Choose a default time frame (e.g., This Week), **OK**.

In this example, when you single-click the flag icon next to a message, the follow-up date will be set for this week. Your Tasks, To-Do Bar, and For Follow Up folder will be populated. If the message is deleted from the Inbox, it's deleted everywhere.

Adjust Time for Default Reminder

In the example above, Outlook will remind me to do something a week from today. My default reminder is set to pop up at 8:00AM. I can change this if needed.

1. Click the **Tools** menu, **Options**, **Preferences** tab.

2. Under Tasks, choose the **Reminder time**.

If you want to enhance a reminder for a flagged item, right-click the flag, **Add Reminder** (see Figure 20 on page 43).

Remove a Flag

To remove a flag, click it if the work is complete. Otherwise, right-click and **Clear Flag**.

Flag Outgoing Messages for Follow-Up

You can flag outgoing messages for follow-up for yourself, the recipient, or both. Create a new message as you normally would:

- For simple reminders: click the **Follow Up** flag, and choose when you want to be reminded by clicking the appropriate flag (e.g., Today, Tomorrow, No Date, etc.).

- For a more detailed follow-up: click the **Follow Up** flag, **Custom**. Choose to remind yourself and/or the recipient, set a specific due date, and create a reminder.

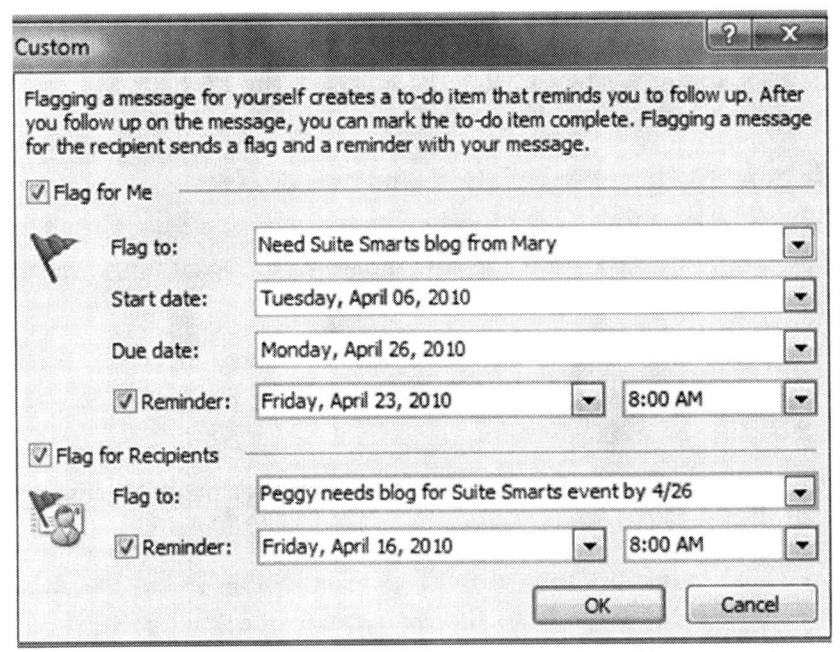

Figure 20. You can type anything in the Flag to box. If you type "next Wednesday" in the Due by or Reminder boxes, Outlook will replace with the right date.

📢 You are not limited to the text in the Flag to drop-down box and can type any text. You can also type words such as "next Wednesday" in the date fields and Outlook will replace with the actual date.

Flag Message for Your Benefit

When you send a message that you need to remember later, flag it and indicate when you'd like to be reminded.

Flag Message for Recipients to See

Messages flagged for the recipient will show a flag and a special message on the InfoBar in the Reading Pane and at the top of the message when they

|43

open it. These messages don't get added to the recipient's to-do lists automatically, but the reminder will appear at the designated time.

Flag Message with Reminders for You and Recipient

With some messages, you want to put a reminder in place for your benefit and the recipient's. When you flag the message, the **Flag for Me** and the **Flag for Recipients** boxes should be ticked.

Respond to Flag with Delete, Complete, or Clear

Flagged text appears in the InfoBar above a message (the shaded bar just above the To or From line). You can sort the view by Flag column to stack all flagged messages together.

When the work is complete (or no longer needed), double-click the message to open it in the For Follow Up folder (or find it on the To-Do Bar), and decide the next best step.

- **Delete.** Delete it only if you no longer need it nor a record of it.
- **Finish.** Click the flag or right-click and click **Complete.** If you mark it Complete, it'll display in the To-Do Bar or Tasks with a strikethrough to indicate you're done. If the work is not marked Complete on its due date, it'll automatically move to the following day and turn red.
- **Change your mind.** Right-click and click **Clear Flag**. When you clear the flag, there will be no indication that you ever followed up on it.

If you receive an email response to a flagged message, you can remove the flag by right-clicking on the InfoBar and clicking **Open Original Flagged Message**. Then click the **Follow Up** flag and **Clear Flag**.

Hide Flagged Messages

I keep my Inbox to one screen so I can always feel confident that nothing's slipped. I changed how I view the Inbox and hid the flagged messages. This way, I won't see them until I need to, based on the reminder date I set (the reminder will still pop up).

1. From the Inbox, click the **View** menu, **Arrange by, Custom, Filter, More Choices**.
2. Tick the box, **Only items which**, and choose **have no flag** in the drop-down list. Click **OK** until you're back in the Inbox. All messages with flags will be hidden.

📣 *Anytime you want to see all of the messages you've flagged, click the For Follow Up folder.*

Fifth Method: Filing the Keepers

If all is going as planned, you've streamlined your Inbox by reducing junk email, redirected some messages with rules, filtered messages with categories, and hidden messages that are flagged for follow up.

By now, you should have also created file folders for the messages you want to keep. Now is a good time to get into another meeting with your Inbox and spend some time moving them. If you want to move several messages that are not together, hold down the **Ctrl** key and click around. Then drag all of them to the appropriate folder. If the messages are together, click the first one and hold down the **Shift** key before you click the last one. With all of them selected, drag them to the folder.

📣 *If the folder you want to drop the messages into is collapsed, don't let go of the mouse. Just hover it over the folder, and it'll expand.*

Find Messages Fast

There are several ways to find a message you've sent, received, or archived.

Instant Search Box

An Instant Search Box is at the top of any Mail view. It's enabled automatically if you use Windows® Vista with Service Pack 1 or higher. If not, you'll be prompted to download the Windows Search software.

1. Click the folder you want to search (e.g., Sent folder).

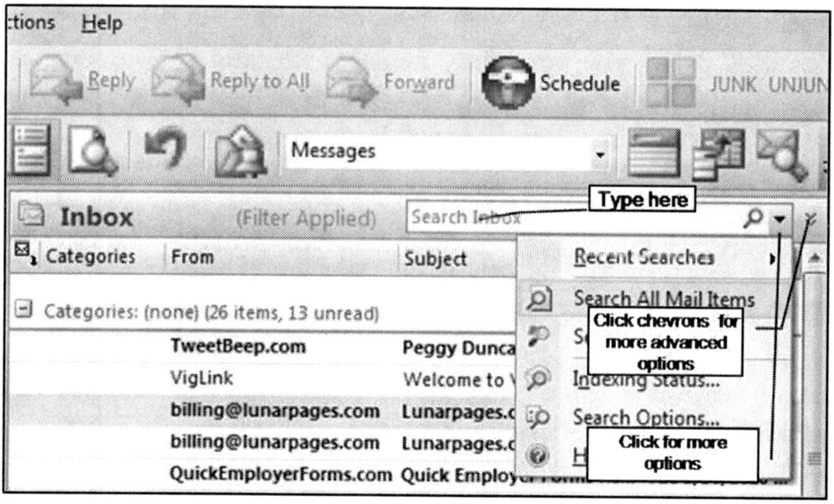

Figure 21. The Instant Search Box displays at the top of any Mail folder.

2. Type a word or phrase in the text box and Outlook will start looking (wait a few seconds even after you see a notice that no matches were found). A list of matching terms should display with the search words highlighted.

When I started using the Instant Search Box, items that I knew were in my calendar did not show up in results. You should do a test to see if you'll need to rebuild the search catalog. If you have a similar problem, first check to make sure Search is enabled (click the **Tools** menu, point to **Instant Search**, and click **Search Options**. Make sure all the boxes are ticked. In the Instant Search Pane at the bottom of the dialog box, I ticked to check **All folders**. If everything is enabled, you'll have to rebuild your search catalog. You should only have to do this once (I think). See instructions on rebuilding the search catalog on page 47.

3. Expand your search if you need to by clicking **Try searching again in All Mail Items** at the end of the first set of results. You can

narrow your search further by clicking the drop-down link on the search box and choosing **Search Options**. Also try clicking the chevrons at the end of the search box for even more options. Click **Add Criteria** and choose.

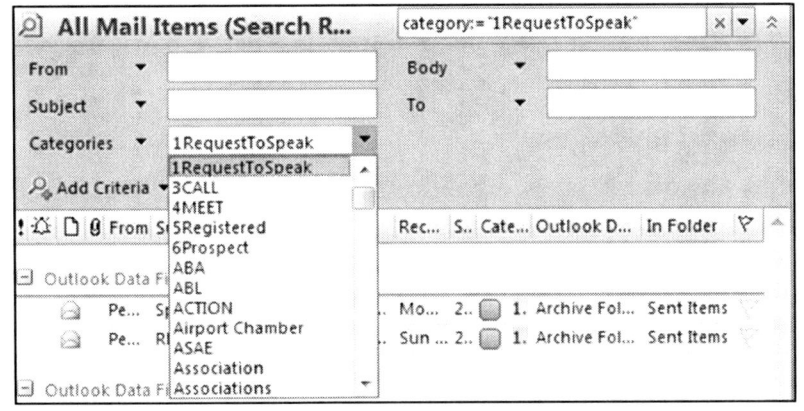

Figure 22. Click the chevrons for a more detailed search box and click **Add Criteria** *for more options such as by Category.*

4. Click **X** beside the search box to clear results.

Rebuild the Search Catalog

If you're not having any luck with search results for something that you know is in Outlook, you'll need to rebuild the search catalog or index.

1. Exit Outlook. Click the **Start** button, **Control Panel**. In Windows Vista, click **System Maintenance, Indexing Options** (if you use the Classic view, double-click Indexing Options). (If you use Windows XP, on the Control Panel under **See Also**, click **Other Control Panel Options, Indexing Options**.)

2. Click **Advanced, Rebuild**. (Be aware that it took about three hours for my system to notify me that it was complete. Then it took about another two hours to finish all indexing.

📢 *If for any reason your Instant Search Box still isn't finding what you need, use Advanced Find to search for words in frequently-used text fields (see more on page 53).*

Find Messages Addressed to You

If you get Cc'd on a lot of messages, you can quickly separate them from the ones addressed to you on the To line. Click Inbox or any folder, and type this command in the Instant Search Box: **to:yourname**.

📢 *You can also create a rule that will send these messages to a designated Read folder.*

Find Unread Messages

To view unread messages, scroll to the Current View Pane in the Navigation Pane and tick **Unread Messages in This Folder**. Or click the folder you want to check, and type **read:no** in the Instant Search Box.

Find Messages With Attachments

If you ever need to find messages that have attachments, select the folder you want to check, and type **hasattachments:true** in the Instant Search Box.

Find Messages from a Sender

You can find all messages from a particular sender by right-clicking on one of their closed messages, point to **Find All**, and click **Messages from Sender**.

If you're in an open message, click **Related** in the *Find group* (on the **Message** tab), and click **Messages from Sender**. When you see the message you want, double-click it to open.

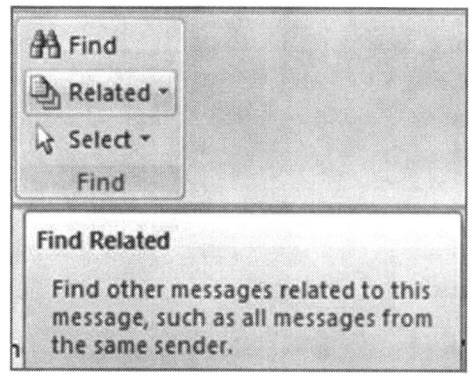

Figure 23. This shortcut to find related messages is only visible when you're inside an open message.

📣 *You can find messages from people in Contacts. Open the contact, click* **Activities** *(in the Show group), click the down arrow next to* **All Items**, *and click* **E-mail** *(messages will start to appear but not always instantly).*

Find Related Messages

You can find related messages that have the same subject line. This is especially handy when you've been out of the office and a lengthy conversation thread has resulted from one message. Right-click on one of the messages in the thread, point to **Find All**, and click **Related Messages**.

If one of the messages is open, click **Related** in the *Find group*, **Related Messages** (on the **Message** tab). When you see the message you want, double-click it to open.

Find Messages by Conversation Topic

You can also view all messages that have the same subject line by conversation topic. I don't use this view because it also shows messages that don't have a thread and can get too confusing to look at.

1. Click the **View** menu, point to **Arrange By, Conversation**.
2. Click the down arrow on the left, next to the message to view the thread.

Define Your Own Views

In addition to using default views in the Current View Pane, you can create your own views with any sorting and filters already applied. (You'll learn more about Define Views beginning on page 122.)

Search Folders

Another excellent option for displaying messages that meet a certain criteria is the Search Folders located near the bottom of the folder list in the Navigation Pane. A search folder isn't a folder, but rather a saved search, and is not to be confused with the Instant Search Box. Outlook comes with default search folders, and you can also build your own.

Default Search Folders

When you click to expand Search Folders, by default, you'll see Categorized Mail, Large Mail, and Unread Mail. If you click either of these, Outlook will display the messages (not just the ones in the Inbox) that match the criteria that has been added.

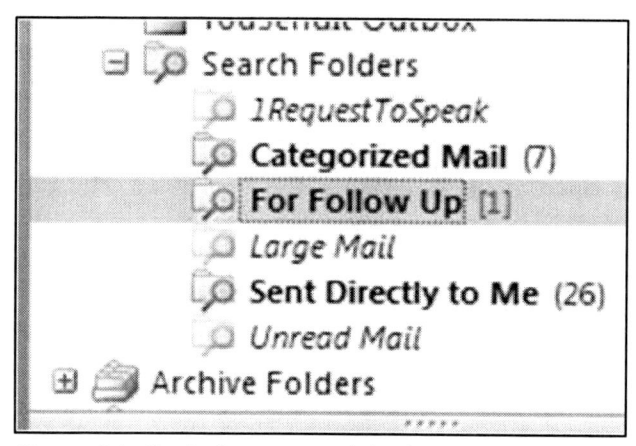

```
    Search Folders
        1RequestToSpeak
        Categorized Mail (7)
        For Follow Up [1]
        Large Mail
        Sent Directly to Me (26)
        Unread Mail
    Archive Folders
```

Figure 24. Outlook comes with built-in Search Folders. You can also build your own.

For Follow Up Search Folder

The For Follow Up folder is a search folder that shows all flagged messages. If you don't see it, it's easy to create one. Right-click on **Search Folders, New Search Folder**, click **Mail flagged for follow up, OK**. Drag this folder to your Favorite Folders.

Create More Search Folders

To view more built-in searches that aren't visible by default, right-click **Search Folders** in the Navigation Pane, **New Search Folder**. The following example shows you how to use one.

In the following example, you'll view all the messages from your boss.

1. Right-click **Search Folders**, click **New Search Folder** (or click the File menu, point to New, click Search Folder).

2. Under *Mail from People and Lists*, double-click **Mail from specific people**, find the name and double-click it, **OK**.

From now on, anytime you need to quickly display all messages from your boss, you'll click this search folder. If you ever need to delete this search or rename it, right-click and **Delete**. Deleting the folder does not delete the messages that are shown in it.

Build Your Own Search Folders

The ability to customize the default search folders is limited because you can only alter the criteria that was included when it was created. However, you can create your own search folders from scratch and have more flexibility.

In this example, you can create a search folder to make it easy to display messages received that have been flagged for follow up and that have come from a particular person, say a boss. (Learn how someone can flag a message they're sending you beginning on page 42).

1. Right-click **Search Folders**, click **New Search Folder** (or click the File menu, point to New, click Search Folder).

2. Scroll down to the bottom of the New Search Folder dialog box, and click **Create a custom Search Folder**. To specify criteria, click **Choose**, give the folder a meaningful name, click **Criteria**.

3. On the **Messages** tab, the boss's email address goes on the **From** line. Your email address goes on the **Sent To** line.

4. On the **More Choices** tab, tick **Only items which**, and choose **are flagged by someone else**.

📢 You can add a category to filter email based on any you've created. And on the Advanced tab, click the Field button for hundreds of other attributes.

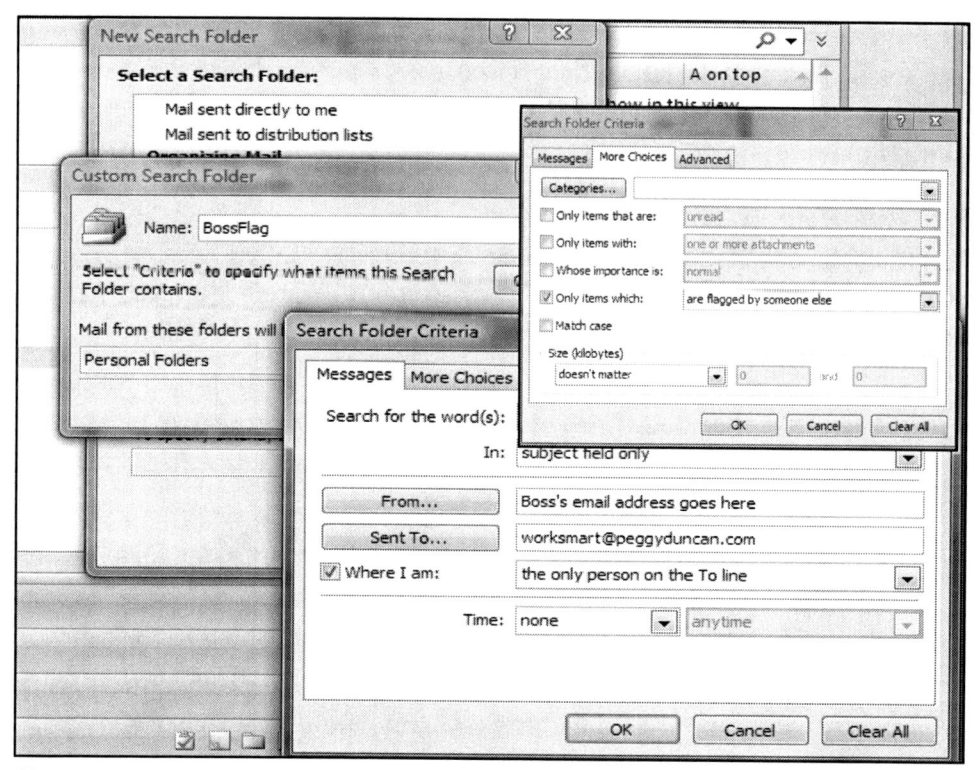

Figure 25. You can create and customize search folders to suit your needs. Click through the other options and play with this.

Create a Search Folder for a Category

If you've created categories for messages you receive (on page 35), you can create a search folder for it.

1. From the Inbox, click the **Edit** menu, **Categorize**, **Create Category Search Folder**. Categorized mail will be selected, click **Choose**.

2. Tick the appropriate category and choose a color box and shortcut key (optional), **OK**.

🔊 *If you need quicker access to this category, drag it from Search Folders to Favorite Folders at the top of the Inbox Folder List.*

Change a Search Folder

Once you set the criteria for a Search Folder, you can change it. Right-click on it, and click **Customize this Search Folder**.

Delete a Search Folder

When you no longer need a search folder, click it and **Delete**. The messages displayed in the folder will remain on your computer.

Advanced Find

The Advanced Find command can help you locate Outlook items quickly. I used this a lot in previous versions, but now I use the Instant Search Box. Click the folder you want to search (e.g., Sent). Click the **Tools** menu, **Instant Search**, **Advanced Find** (or **Ctrl+Shift+F**), or click the Advanced Search toolbar button.

In Figure 26, I was looking for an email message I'd sent to a friend of mine with the name and phone number of a plumber. I couldn't remember the plumber's name, but I knew it was in that email I'd sent.

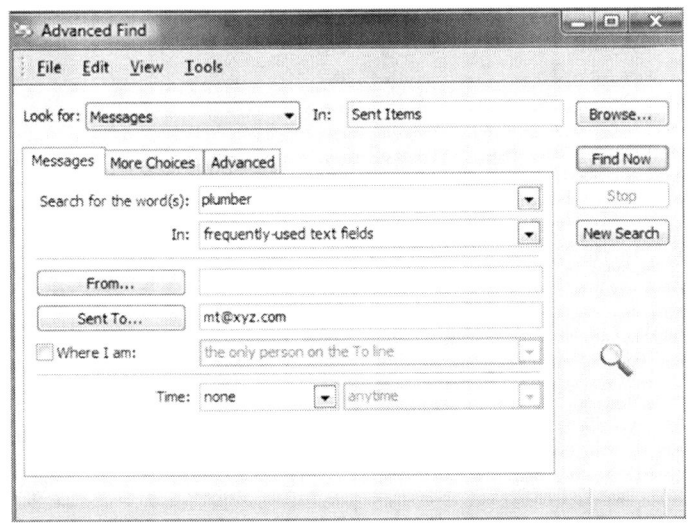

Figure 26. Sent Items appeared in this Advanced Find dialog box because I clicked the folder first. I chose "frequently-used text fields" so Outlook would search everywhere in the message. (The new Instant Search Box has replaced the need for Advanced Find in m instances.)

Sort Messages

You can rearrange how your messages appear in any folder, using different views for each one. For example, you might want to view the messages currently in your Inbox by Date, but you'd rather see your Deleted Items folder by Subject.

1. Sort messages by field (From, Subject, Date Received, etc.) by clicking the appropriate column heading. For example, if you want to sort messages by subject, click the **Subject** heading. To reverse the order, click Subject again.

   To sort a message by more than one column, hold down the **Shift** key and click another column heading.

2. If you don't see the field you want to sort by, right-click any heading, and drag it from the **Field Chooser**.

   Figure 27. From inside your Inbox, you can click on the column headings and sort your messages quickly.

Field Chooser

Anytime you need a column header in Outlook that doesn't appear by default, you can add it with Field Chooser.

In this example, the Categories column will be added. Right-click the column header, and click **Field Chooser**. Click the drop-down for more options on where to look. In this example, I chose **Frequently-used fields**. Scroll to find **Categories**, click and drag it to the column header (for this exercise, put it next to Full Name), and release the mouse.

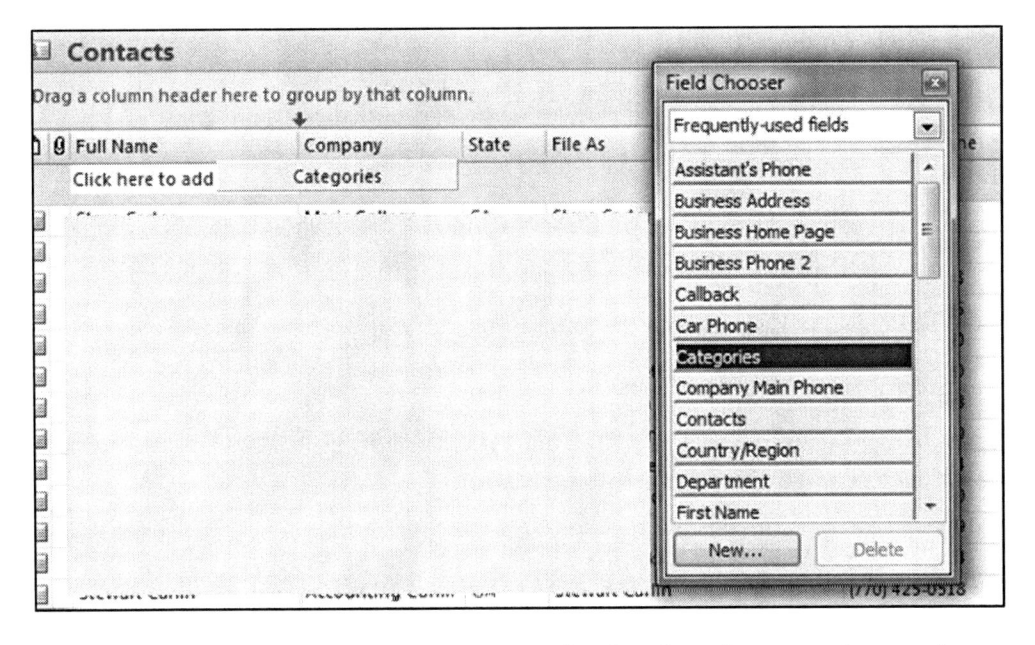

Figure 28. When adding a field to the column header, the red arrow indicates where it'll land when you release the mouse. To remove a column, click it and drag off the header.

Arrange By

Whichever view you use, you can group and sort messages using the **Arrange By** command on the **View** menu. I separate my messages using categories. Messages with categories applied to them appear at the bottom of my Inbox, and the messages with no categories appear at the top in Date order. I usually turn off the option to **Show in Groups** because I want all of my messages in one, clean line (I keep my Inbox to one screen).

Sort Messages by More Than One Column

You can sort your messages by more than one column. One way is to click on the first column you want to sort by, hold down the **Shift** key, and click the next column to sort by. Two other ways to sort by multiple columns include customizing the current view and using the Group By Box.

Customize Current View

1. From any Mail folder, right-click on any column heading, click **Customize Current View, Sort**. In the **Sort items by** box, click a field to sort by.

2. Click **Ascending** or **Descending** for the sort order. To sort by an additional field, click a field in the **Then by** box. Click **OK**.

📣 *To remove sorting, click on the column you no longer want to sort by.*

Group By Box

The Group By Box allows you to display messages in groups based on multiple columns (see page 156 for more information).

Messages You RECEIVE

Adjust the New Message Alert

By default, a notification box appears when most new messages arrive. It'll display enough information about the message so you can determine whether to deal with it right then, delete it, or leave it alone for now. You can turn this feature off or change how it works.

1. Click the **Tools** menu, **Options**, **Preferences** tab, **E-mail Options**, **Advanced E-mail Options**.

2. In the *When new items arrive in my Inbox* section, untick **Display a New Mail Desktop Alert** if you don't want to be notified.

If you decide to keep the notification, you can change how it appears.

3. Click the **Desktop Alert Settings** button, and make desired changes. Click the **Preview** button to see how your alert will appear.

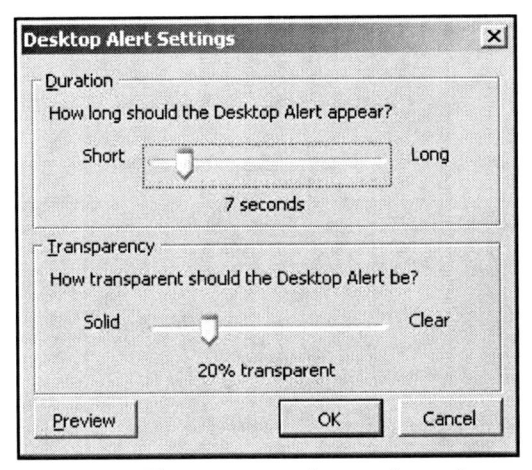

Figure 29. This setting is the one I use for new message alerts.

When your email alert appears, if you click the **x**, you can delete the message without opening it. If you click the link to the message, it'll open.

Turn Off the Ding

If you don't want a sound to distract you every time you receive a new message, you can deactivate it.

1. Click the **Tools** menu, **Options**, **Preferences** tab, **E-mail Options**, **Advanced E-mail Options**.

2. In the *When new items arrive in my Inbox* section, untick **Play a sound**.

Keep Read Messages Bold

It was driving me crazy that every time I clicked on a message in the Inbox to read it in the Reading Pane, it would lose the bold formatting that denotes an unread message. I turned this feature off and my message stays bold unless I open it.

1. Click the **Tools** menu, **Options**, the **Other** tab, **Reading Pane**.
2. Untick **Mark item as read when selection changes**, click **OK**.

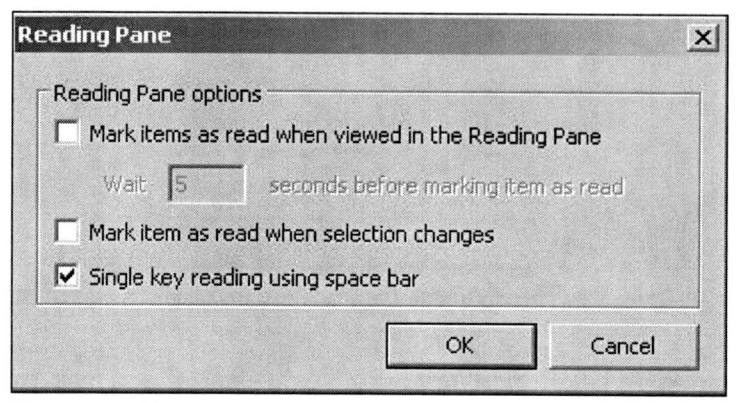

Figure 30. If you want your message to remain bold after viewing it in the Reading Pane (without opening it), change the option here.

Define Large Messages

You can stop messages over a certain size from automatically downloading into your Inbox. Once set up, the message header will download so you'll know who sent the message, what it's about, and how large it is. Then you can determine if you need it or not. This is especially handy when you're travelling and using a slower connection speed.

1. Click the **Tools** menu, point to **Send/Receive**, point to **Send/Receive Settings** (it's at the bottom of the Send/Receive menu). Click **Define Send/Receive Groups** (or press Ctrl+Alt+S).
2. Select **All Accounts**, click the **Edit** menu and make your changes.

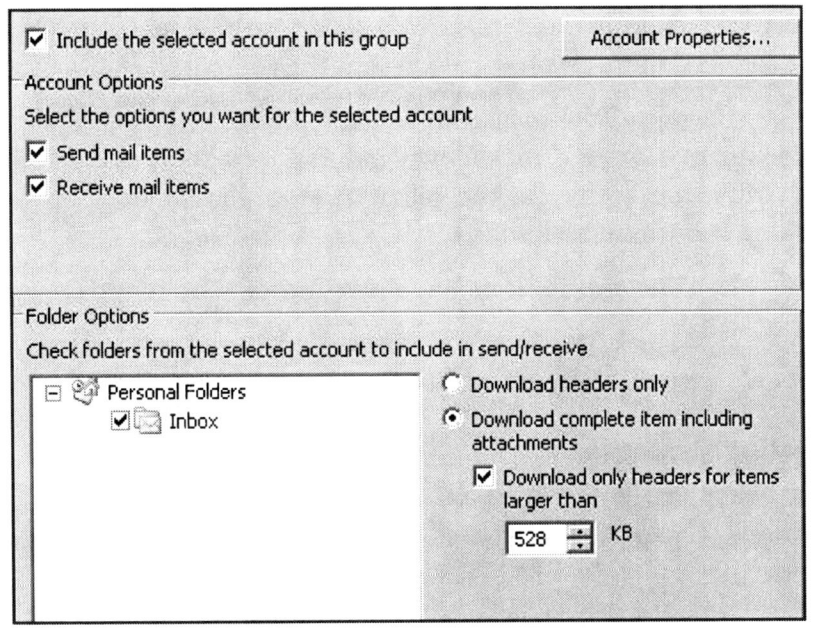

Figure 31. I set Outlook up to not automatically download any messages larger than 528 KB.

3. Tick the box, **Download only headers for items larger than**, and choose desired size.

Here's how this works. Only a header will download from the server when the message exceeds the size you designated. If you decide to download the complete message, right-click it in the Inbox and click either to **Mark to Download Message(s)** or mark it for deletion. If you choose to delete the message, it will be marked, and during the next Send/Receive, it will be deleted from the server and from your Inbox. If you choose to download, it will be marked, and during the next Send/Receive, the full message will download from the server and appear in your Inbox.

Block Automatic Download of Pictures

To help protect your privacy and combat Web beacons, Outlook is configured by default to not automatically download pictures and other content from the Internet when you display a message. (A Web beacon notifies the Web server when you read or preview a message, validating the email address and often resulting in more junk messages being sent to you.) If an e-mail message tries to connect unannounced to a Web server on the Internet, Outlook blocks that connection until you decide to view the content.

To download the images in a single message, right-click on the InfoBar inside the message and click **Download Pictures**. You can turn this feature off and automatically receive the pictures. (You should have up to date virus protection if you turn this off.)

1. Click the **Tools** menu, **Trust Center, Automatic Download**.
2. Untick the **Don't download pictures automatically in HTML e-mail messages or RSS items** check box.

Deleting Messages

The delete key is the most used key on my keyboard when I'm checking messages. Here are three things I changed in Outlook for handling deleted items.

Deleted Items Folder

Messages pile into my Deleted Items folder every day. Instead of having Outlook empty it automatically when I exit, I set it up to AutoArchive every three weeks and permanently delete older messages (see more information on AutoArchiving beginning on page 168).

Check to see if Outlook is set up to automatically empty the Deleted Items folder every time you exit. Play it safe and turn this feature off. (The Deleted Items folder is located in the Navigation Pane just above the Drafts and Inbox folders.)

1. Click the **Tools** menu, **Options, Other** tab.
2. Untick **Empty the Deleted Items folder upon exiting**.

You can bypass the Deleted Items folder and permanently delete an item from your computer by holding down the **Shift** key as you click **Delete**. To make this feature even more convenient, you may want to turn off the warning box that pops up every time you attempt to delete an item. If so, on the same **Other** tab, click **Advanced Options,** and untick the box next to **Warn before permanently deleting items.**

🔊 *Also refer to the information on AutoArchiving beginning on page 168 for another option on deleting items.*

Delete from the Deleted Items Folder

Anytime you delete an item in Outlook, if you don't hold down the Shift key as you click Delete, it will go into the Deleted Items folder. To empty it, right-click on the **Deleted Items** folder (located in the Navigation Pane), and click **Empty "Deleted Items" Folder**.

Recover Deleted Items

If you accidentally delete an email message, a contact, calendar item, or task, go to the Mail view, and look in your Deleted Items folder.

If you permanently deleted the item (held down the Shift key when you clicked Delete) and are on a Microsoft Exchange Server, you can retrieve it (if your administrator enabled this feature).

1. In the Navigation Pane, click **Deleted Items**.
2. Click the **Tools** menu, **Recover Deleted Items**.
3. Click the item you want to retrieve, and click **Recover Selected Items**. The item will appear in your Deleted Items folder.

Editing Messages

Edit Subject Line

You probably receive many messages with poor subject lines. Some don't provide enough information to let you know what the message is about, and others have absolutely nothing to do with the message.

You can edit the subject line of a message someone sends you. Before you file it away, change the subject line so you'll recognize the message later.

1. Click anywhere in the subject text and make desired changes. (To select the entire subject line, triple-click it.)
2. Close the message, and click **Yes** to save your changes.

Edit a Message Before You File It

You can add a comment to a message before you file it.

1. From the open message, click the **Message** tab, **Other Actions**, **Edit Message**.

2. Click inside the message, and add your comments (I sometimes precede my edits with "Note from Peggy").

3. Click the **Move to Folder** command (or **Ctrl+Shift+V**), **Other folder**, and file the message as you normally would.

Saving Messages

Save a Message Outside of Outlook

You may need to save email messages outside of Outlook. You can do this and also keep any attachments with the message. (If you want to remove an attachment before you save a message, either right-click on it and click Remove or click it and Delete).

1. From an open message, click the **Office** button, **Save As, Save As**.

2. Click the **Save as type** drop-down box (located at the bottom of the Save as dialog box), and change from Text Only to **Outlook Message Format** (.msg extension, not Unicode).

3. Save the file as you normally would. Later, you can open the message as you would any file (you don't have to open from Outlook, but Outlook needs to be open for the best results).

📣 *If you have a message you send often, create it and add the text, your signature, attachments, etc. Then save it in the .msg format somewhere you can get to quickly (e.g., on your Desktop or Taskbar). Anytime you need to email it, double-click it to open, address it, and send as you normally would. This works better than a draft because your original message stays intact and in place so you can use it again and again.*

Save Multiple Messages as One File

Once a project is over, you may want to save all the related messages as one text file.

1. Select multiple messages as you normally would, and click the **File** menu, **Save As**.
2. In the Save As box, choose where you want to save the file, name it, change **Save as type** to **Text Only (*txt)**, **Save**. Then delete the original messages.

📢 You can select multiple messages that are together if you click the first one to select it, hold down the **Shift** key and click the last one in the group (all messages between the two clicks will be selected). If the messages aren't together, hold down the **Ctrl** key and click on the ones you want to include in the selection.

Keep Messages on the Server

Normally, when you check email, messages come in from your ISP into Outlook and is deleted from their servers. Sometimes it could be beneficial if the messages remain on the server (e.g., when you're travelling and using Webmail on different computers).

1. Click the **Tools** menu, **Account Settings**, double-click the account to change, **More Settings, Advanced**.

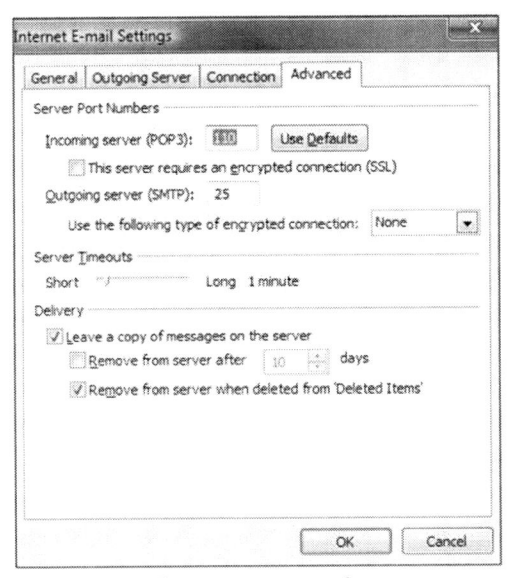

Figure 32. You can opt to leave messages on the server when you're travelling and using different computers.

2. Tick the boxes, **Leave a copy of messages on the server** and **Remove from server when deleted from 'Deleted Items'** or choose a certain number of days to leave them there.

📢 *Remember to reverse this change when you get back to your normal routine.*

Printing Messages

You should be very selective about what you print because it adds to clutter and we're all going green. You can save ink, paper, and trees by printing only what you need.

Print Portion of a Message

Help save the environment by printing only the part of a message you need.

1. Open the message and click **Other Actions** (located in the Actions group), **View in Browser**. Wait for the message to open in your default browser.

2. Select the part of the message you want to print.

3. Click the **File** menu, **Print, Selection, OK**.

📢 *To use this feature, you must have the 2007 Microsoft Office Suite Service Pack 2 (SP2). If you don't see View in Browser, you should download this update on the Microsoft.com Web site. This technique doesn't work on graphic files such as an invitation someone has embedded in the message.*

Use Out of Office Email Feature

If you're on a Microsoft Exchange Server, you can use the Out of Office Assistant to create and send autoresponses back to people who send you messages, letting them know your status.

My advice is not to use this feature if you're in an environment that gets a lot of spam because you'd autorespond to spammers and now they know your email address is valid. And not to mention that now they know you're out of the country for two weeks!

1. From the Mail folder, click the **Tools** menu, **Out of Office Assistant**.

2. Complete the information in the dialog box.

3. Later, when you open Outlook, you'll be asked if you want to turn off the Out of Office message.

If you're not on an Exchange server, you can set up an out of office autoresponder with your Internet service provider. Instructions for doing this should be on their Web site.

Subscribe to RSS Feeds

If you're subscribing to RSS Feeds, you can bring them into Outlook. You'll need the URL of the feed to set this up.

1. Click the **Tools** menu, **Account Settings**, **RSS Feeds** tab, **New**.
2. Type or paste the URL (**Ctrl+V**) of the RSS Feed. In case you're interested, the feed to my award-winning technology blog, SUITE MINUTE, is http://suiteminute.com/feed/.
3. Click **Add, OK**.

If you subscribed to my blog feed, every time I write a new post, you'll receive it directly into your RSS Feed folder that's in Outlook by default.

Messages You SEND

Create Better Messages

Before you send your next email missive, consider the P-E-G-G-Y model for creating better messages.

> **P**lan your message and be clear on its purpose.
> **E**xplain who you are and what you need.
> **G**ive them everything they need so they can help you.
> **G**et to the point quickly, and thank them in advance.
> **Y**ield to the temptation to say more or send to everyone.

|65

- **Think first, then write.** If you're upset, angry, or emotional about a topic, wait before you start to write. Don't send a message you could be sorry for later. It's always a good idea to complete the To line last and save the message in Drafts until you're ready.

- **Address the message appropriately.** The person that assumes the action is on the To line. Anyone on the Cc or Bcc lines will assume no action.

- **Write descriptive subject lines.** If you write a good subject line, recipients will fully understand what your message is about before they open it. Just as a headline in a media release, the subject line of your message should tell the whole story. Make it specific to the message (e.g., not "WordPress Bootcamp," but "Please send your handout for the next WordPress Bootcamp.")

You will especially appreciate good subject lines once your message is filed and you need to retrieve it.

- **Make your subject line match the message.** If you're in the habit of pulling up an old message someone sent you months ago, then hitting Reply to ask them something that's totally unrelated to the old message, stop! The subject line and the body of a message go together so they should match!

Would you send a letter to someone referencing one thing but then proceeding to discuss something completely different? No? Then why do this with email? Plus, people are prioritizing their email based on the subject, and they may want to file it to use later (see page 61 on editing the subject line).

- **Limit messages to one topic.** It'll be easier for the recipient to prioritize messages and file them later if you limit messages to one topic. If you add various topics within one message, mention it in the subject line, and number each new topic with 1), 2), or something similar.

- **Create a company-wide classification system.** As a team, your company could develop words that introduce subject lines that make it obvious at a glance what the message is about or the action to take. It's important that everyone knows what the codes mean. Some codes are as follows. You'll also create more of your own.

EXAMPLE

Subject: CALL: Betty Johnson at XYZ to discuss speaking at convention.

CODE	DESCRIPTION
ACTION	The recipient has work to do.
CALL	The recipient is going to have to call someone.
END	Use at the end of a subject line when it includes everything you had to say. No need to open message.
FYI	For Your Information. No action needed. Message is for information purposes only.
IRN	Immediate response needed.
MEET	Another dreaded meeting notice.
NRN	No response is necessary.
rBig	Reply to everyone who is copied.
rSmall	Reply only to sender.

If you send messages outside your organization, be sure to use coding that most people would understand, such as FYI or END.

- **Use a salutation that fits.** As in a letter, you should address the recipient according to your relationship. If it's someone you know, it's appropriate to address by the first name. If it's someone you haven't met, you'll want to use Mr., Ms., etc. Don't send a message without a salutation because it'll come across as a demand.

- **Identify yourself upfront.** You want your message opened. Let people know who you are, how you know them, where you met, who referred you, etc. If you've met them before, don't assume they'll remember. If I've been referred by someone, I put that name in the subject line.

- **Be thorough but brief.** Your message should be brief, but make sure you include enough information to tell the whole story. If your point will require a detailed explanation and you know it's going to generate a lot of questions, a phone call will work better. Then you could follow up the phone call with email.

  Ask for what you want upfront, using short sentences and short paragraphs. Break up your paragraphs with the start of each new thought, just as you would in normal writing.

- **Make important information stand out.** If you need something to stand out, make it bold, surround it with asterisks, or put it in a separate paragraph. If it's a deadline, make it bold and also put it in a separate paragraph at the beginning of your message. Avoid using excessive exclamation points and don't use underlines (because it'll look like a hyperlink).

- **Close your message politely.** End your message the way you would in a letter, although not necessarily with the same verbiage.

Grammar Rules Apply

You should treat email as you would any other form of business communication, taking care to convey the right message quickly with the right tone, and using standard rules of grammar and punctuation. You will be judged accordingly.

- **Spelling Check.** You may want to run Spelling Check on messages before sending. Click the **Tools** menu, **Options**, **Spelling** tab. Tick **Always check spelling before sending** box.

- **Custom Dictionary.** Once you turn on Spelling Check, you may want to add your industry or company jargon to the dictionary so your software will recognize certain words, acronyms, etc., and not mark them as errors. In the same dialog box as the previous tip, click **Spelling and AutoCorrection, Custom Dictionaries, Edit Word List**, and type a word or phrase you want to add, pressing **Enter** after each.

- **Capitalization.** Most people know not to use ALL CAPS in email communication because it's the equivalent of screaming at a person when you're face to face. Capitalizing a heading or one or two words is acceptable, but not entire paragraphs.

  You can turn off the feature that automatically capitalizes the first letter of sentences. Click the **Tools** menu, **Options, Spelling** tab. Click **Spelling and AutoCorrection, Proofing** (on the left), **AutoCorrect Options**. Untick the box next to **Capitalize first letter of sentences**.

📣 *For more grammar help, right-click a word in the body of your message and choose Look Up for a definition, Synonyms for similar words, or Thesaurus.*

Add Interest to Your Message with HTML

All (or most) email clients can accept messages using the HyperText Markup Language or HTML (computer language used to create documents on the Web). If you want to insert graphics or use text formatting such as font color, you'll need to use the HTML or Rich Text format. You can also use the HTML format to send newsletters, ads, and so on (see page 89 for information on inserting graphics into a message).

The HTML format also works best for preserving long URLs, regardless of the recipient's mail program.

If you still prefer to use the plain text format, you can change the format from inside a message (open a message, click the **Options** tab and choose from the Format group). You can also change Outlook's options to automatically format your messages in either HTML, Rich Text, or plain text (from Mail view, click the **Tools** menu, **Options, Mail Format** tab, and choose).

Decorations: Designs, Emoticons, and Smileys

People are busy. Email messages are piling in. Your sending messages that are simple, clean, and easy to read will help the recipient go through email quicker.

- **Designs**. This version of Outlook gives you the ability to decorate your messages. I've totally ignored these commands in this book because I don't want you to consider using them. Decorations slow people down. Some of them block the text and distract from your message. If you're using email for business, keep it professional, and save the decorations for your next crafts project. If you would not have letterhead printed with ivy growing down the side or flowers all over it, you shouldn't create email messages with this either. For now, let's ignore the Themes group on the Options tab.

- **Emoticons**. If you received an email message with this in it, **:-O**, would you know it means open-mouthed, surprised? Neither did I, and neither will most people. Emoticons are those facial expressions made by a certain series of keystrokes. Most often, they produce an image that can be read with your face turned sideways. If you're emailing your friends, and you know they understand what they mean, then go for it. But in business, it's best to omit them.

- **Smileys**. Smileys are cartoon-like icons you download and add to your email messages to convey various moods. Like emoticons, these are not appropriate for business use. They're distracting, and you never know how they will translate on the receiving end. Also, many of these free downloads act as spyware (programming that is put on your computer to secretly gather information about you and relay it to advertisers or other interested parties).

Use a Typeface that Fits

You should use a typeface that fits your company. If you're a day care center, a comedian, or you write jokes for a living, you may choose to use a playful typeface such as Comic Sans. Otherwise, use one that's more appropriate for a professional business. The same is true for choosing a typeface for your business card, Web site, brochures, etc.

To change the typeface, click the **Tools** menu, **Options**, **Mail Format** tab, **Stationery and Fonts**, **Font**. Make any adjustments.

Also, under **When replying and forwarding**, click **Font** and change to **Automatic** or **Black**. Keep your messages simple, clean, and easy on the eyes (the default blue ink on replies and forwards is hard on the eyes).

Read more on email and your image beginning on page 76.

Improve the From Line

Another way to help recipients of your messages know who you are (and another great way to self-promote) is to add information they will see on the From line.

📢 *Now is a good time to send a message to yourself so you can see how it looks in the Inbox.*

1. From the Inbox, click the **Tools** menu, **Account Settings**.
2. Double-click the account you want to improve.
3. In the **Your Name** box, add desired information. Mine reads "Peggy Duncan, Personal Productivity Expert."
4. Click **Next**, **Finish**. Change information for each account as needed.

Email Pet Peeves

If left unchecked, spam can drive you nuts, but what about the email messages from people you either want to or have to hear from? Are they doing anything that's making you swear at your computer screen every time you "hear" from them?

Bad email habits are aggravating. They also contribute to email overload. If you change your email habits based on these pet peeves, you'll be well on your way to managing email overload better. And people will look forward to hearing from you.

- **Sending or responding to all to CYA** (cover your butt). Stop sending to all if all do not have a need to know. You wanted to make sure you were covered so you're sending everyone on a list your answer—whether they needed to know or not. Or you're sending a message to everyone because you're too lazy to select the appropriate recipients. And when you're forwarding on top of forwarding, the originator ends up with his own message!

- **Trying to solve complex issues using email.** You're part of a new committee, then the email messages start, back and forth, dizzying speed, the more they come, the more confused you get. Pick up the phone!

- **Replying and leaving the messages messy.** These are those messages you receive loaded with those darn carets (>>>), or pages and pages of email addresses that weren't protected using Bcc. Is it too much to ask for the sender to clean messages before sending it? Would you send a letter out on your company stationery like that? You can get rid of carets by selecting the text, **Ctrl+H** to use the Find and Replace command to find a caret and replace all of them with nothing. You can get rid of all the email addresses just by deleting. Clean it up, then send it.

- **Not matching subject lines to the message.** Don't pull up an old message, hit Reply, and send me a message that has nothing to do with the previous one. Suppose you sent an email message two months ago that said, "The monthly meeting has been cancelled." You pulled up that old message because the email addresses were already in it. But this time, you wanted to let everyone know that coffee and donuts would be served at this month's meeting. At the very least, change the subject line!

- **Using for last-minute cancellations.** Cancelling a meeting at the last minute and letting me know via email. I show up, "Oh, didn't you get my e-mail?" When did you send it? I left my office two hours ago, I don't check email while driving, and now my whole day is shot.

- **Holding up work.** People who wait until the last minute to ask you to do something as if you had nothing else to do. You know the work was in a pile on their desk, and while they were digging for something else, they found it, and sent you an email message, marking it urgent. Then when the deadline isn't met, it's not their fault because they "gave it to you."

- **Not checking email.** You've done your job, and sent an email message to people with information they need. They end up calling you asking for the info because, "I'm too busy to check email. Please always call me with the information or at least call me to let me know you sent it."

- **Asking about it too quickly.** These are the people who'll send you a message, then call you or come by your desk asking if you received it.

- **Not responding.** You send a legitimate email message to someone who has requested information. The message clearly needs a response, but nothing happens. If you're too busy to hit Reply to say "No," you need to examine how you're working. Why did you make me waste your time and mine?

- **Sending one-liners.** "thanks," "Oh, OK." My goodness! You sent an email message to 25 people, and 15 of them sent you a one-liner. Next time, put "No Reply Necessary" at the top.

- **Using underlines.** Don't underline anything in a message (or on a Web page) that's not a hyperlink. I always move the mouse toward it thinking it'll take me somewhere.

- **Replying to my message without the previous message below it or attached to it.** I forgot what I asked about.

- **Using smileys, emoticons.** If you wouldn't put a smiley face or emoticon on your business correspondence, you shouldn't put it in an email message.

- **Updating with Plaxo and similar services.** Those emails from you asking me to update my contact information. I don't even remember who these people are. I went to the Plaxo Web site and opted out of receiving any of these annoying updates. Make sure you opt out all of your email addresses!

- **Using senseless autoresponders.** How about the one that says "Thank you for your email message. I will respond to you as soon as I can." What a complete waste of my time to open this useless response. It's almost like the letter carrier leaving me a message in my mailbox saying, "I picked up your mail today. I'll bring you more when I get it."

- **Using shortcuts to real words.** Words from grown, business people using shortcuts such as "4 u" (instead of "for you"), "Gr8" (for great) in business-related email is not acceptable. Are you lazy, or just can't type or spell? If you wouldn't send a company letter out like that, it shouldn't be in an email message. (This is different from legitimate abbreviations a company may develop such as NRN for No Reply Necessary.)

- **Checking up with read receipt.** As if you're checking up on me to see if I open your message. I don't know why people waste time doing this because most people probably have this feature turned off in their email software.

- **Adding too many attachments.** You should get permission before sending someone an email message with more than two attachments. Instead of sending five PDFs, combine them into one document.

- **Sending an attachment and no message in the body.** Don't do this.

- **Writing too much.** You're sending pages and pages of one conversation and I'm having to dig through it all to figure out what's going on.

- **Not using Bcc.** No Bcc and pages of email addresses in the message. You've exposed your list to all who receive it and you didn't protect our privacy.

- **Passing on hoaxes instead of checking them out first.** What would make you believe that a company would send you $5000 just for sending an email message? Check it out first by typing the main words from the message into the search engine.

- **Not letting recipient know who are you.** People I met briefly sometime ago sending me an email message without reminding me who they are.

- **Sending messages without signature lines.** Your email signature is a great way to let people know more about you, especially when your email address is something like 189bx@stupiddomain.com.

- **Adding me to your email list.** I just met you, barely remember you, and I'm already on your distribution list for your newsletter, thoughts for the day, and news you think I want to know.

- **Using bad grammar and punctuation.** You can't hide behind an administrative assistant to clean up your act, so go take some classes and learn how to write and spell. Some messages are so bad, it's like reading a foreign language, and it wastes my time trying to figure out your mess.

- **Misusing work email.** People sending me non-work-related email from their job. I don't want my name and email address showing up in company reports.

- **Using unprofessional email IDs.** People who send a business message using addresses such as cutesuzy@xx.com; blessd@xx.com; hardliquor@mean.com

I'll repeat: if you pay attention to the pet peeves, you'll send and receive less messages.

What Not to Send Via Email

Email is not always the best way to communicate. Put yourself in the recipient's place, and use your best judgment for each situation. Here is a sample of what not to send using email.

- **Last-minute cancellations.** Some people can't get to email as easily as they can voicemail. If you're cancelling a meeting at the last minute (for email, this is within 24-48 hours of the event), you could send a text message or an email message and ask the recipients to send a confirmation. Then call the people who don't respond.

- **Devastating news.** If you have an employee or a friend you need to deliver bad news to, a phone call will be better. If it's news you have to deliver to a large group, email is more practical.

- **Complex topics or explanations.** When the subject requires explanations that will generate lots of questions, a phone call, face-to-face, or Web meeting is a better solution.

- **Hoaxes.** Before you send a message to all your friends or associates about some terrible thing that could happen to them, or a virus that could wipe out their entire computer system, check it out first (Google it or visit www.Snopes.com).

- **Junk, chain letters, etc.** It's not just you sending your friend a joke he just has to read: it's you and ten other friends. Often, people are too embarrassed to ask you to stop, so I'm asking you. Stop.

Improve Your Image

Communicating via email is quick and easy. But one of its shortcomings is that it doesn't give people you don't know much to go on when judging you or your business.

The Right Email Address

Your email address speaks volumes about who you are and the type of business you run or work for. Which correspondent below will be taken more seriously? Which address suggests the correspondent means business?

pd12@freemail.com – Junk. Delete.

cuteseygirl@freemail.com – You've got to be kidding. Delete.

man12@aol.com – Your business is a hobby. That's too bad. Delete.

worksmart@peggyduncan.com – A company Web site. Hmmm. Must have something to do with working smarter. I'll check this out.

Email Etiquette

When sending messages, the following are factors to consider.

- **Address the message appropriately.** People on the To line will take action. Use the Cc line to copy people for information only, and only when they have a need to know.

- **Send or copy others only on a need to know basis.** Before you click Reply All or put names on the Cc or Bcc lines, ask yourself if all the recipients need the information in your message. If they don't, why send it? Take time to send your messages to the right people.

- **Maintain privacy of email addresses.** If you're sending a message to a group of people and you need to protect the privacy of your list, use Bcc (on page 79).

  Another way to protect the privacy of your email addresses is to avoid giving them to a third party (Evite, or sites with "Send this email to your friends," etc.). Make sure that addresses you willingly hand over to third parties stay with them, especially when the service they're offering is free.

- **Minimize attachments.** You should send an attachment only to people you know or to people who are expecting it.

  The following should be considered as part of your company's email culture.

  o Refrain from sending a message with more than two attachments, unless it's been requested.

  o Take care in giving the attached file(s) a logical name so the recipient knows at a glance the subject and the sender.

  o Mention the attachment, and put a brief description of it inside the body of the message. Remember to actually attach the file. As soon as you type the word "attached" or "attachment," stop right then and do it.

- **Don't overuse the high priority option.** If you overuse this feature, few people will take it seriously. A better solution is to use descriptive subject lines that explain exactly what a message is about.

- **Don't overuse the Delivery and Read receipt message options.** This feature usually annoys your recipient, and it adds to email clutter. And besides, most of your recipients probably have this featured turned off (**Tools, Options, Email Options, Tracking Options, Never send a response**).

Send a Message to a Contact

If a person is in your Contacts, type the name on the **To** line, and Outlook will find the email address. If you have two people with the same name, Outlook will let you resolve (double-click the one you want). (The issue with the contact's fax number showing up in the To field was resolved in Outlook 2003. The fax number will show up in the list of possible addresses for the contact, but you'll be able to choose an email address to use.)

If you're looking at a closed contact in Contact view (and you've added the email address), you can drag it to the Mail folder or icon to create a message addressed to the contact.

Use an Email Address that Pops Up

When you type a name or email address on the To, Cc, or Bcc lines, Outlook will display a list of choices (called AutoComplete or AutoSuggest). To use an email address that pops up, either click it or use your up or down arrow keys on the keyboard to select it, and press **Enter**.

Delete Email Addresses that Pop Up on To Line

When you're addressing an email message and Outlook suggests recipients, you can delete all or some of these names from the cache so they won't appear. Use the up or down arrow keys on your keyboard to highlight the unwanted address and **Delete** (the address will remain in Contacts, but won't be suggested to you by Outlook).

🔊 I like this feature, but if you don't, you can turn it off. From the Inbox, click the **Tools** menu, **Options**. On the **Preferences** tab, click **Email Options, Advanced Email Options**. Then, untick the **Suggest names while completing To, Cc, Bcc fields** box.

Send a Message to Multiple People with Bcc

When you send messages to multiple people, use the Bcc option to keep your email addresses private. Create a new message, click the **Options** tab, **Show Bcc**. To use this feature, create a new message as you normally would. Put your email address on the **To** line, and add the recipient email addresses on the **Bcc** line.

When the message arrives, each recipient will only see his or her name in the message. If anyone clicks Reply to All, other recipient names will not show, and only the original sender will receive the reply.

🔊 An email address needs to be on the To line so your message does not look like spam to the receiving system.

Send a Message from the Contacts Folder

You can also send a message from the Contacts folder.

- Drag the closed contact item to the Inbox folder or icon in the Navigation Pane.

- Or right-click the Contact, **Create, New Message to Contact**.

- Or click once on the contact, click the drop-down arrow next to the **New** toolbar button, **Mail Message**.

If the contact item is open, click the **E-mail** command (inside the Communicate Group).

Send a Message to a Category

Once you've assigned a category to your contacts (the same way you do for messages), there are several ways to send a message to everyone. You'll have to filter out the ones with an email address. In the first example, you have email addresses for everyone in a category, but in the second example, you don't.

You Have All Email Addresses
You're sending the message to everyone in the category

1. Click **By Category** in the Contacts Navigation Pane under *Current View*. Find the category you want to send the email to and click its header.

2. With all the contacts in that category selected, drag them to the Mail folder or icon. A new message will open with your contacts on the To line.

3. Click one of the email addresses to select it, then **Ctrl+A** to select all of them. Drag them down to the **Bcc** line. (Actually, I drag the email addresses to the body of the message and leave them there until I've finished writing. This way I won't make a mistake and send the message before I'm ready.)

You Don't Have All Email Addresses
You need to filter and send to certain people

Example: I'm sending a message to everyone in my *Media* category, State of *Georgia*, with email addresses.

1. From Contacts, click **Advanced Find** (on the Standard toolbar). On the **More Choices** tab, type "Media" in the Categories box, or click to find it. (You can add multiple categories here and separate by a comma.)

2. On the **Advanced** tab, choose **Field** (e-mail), **Condition** (is not empty), and choose **Field** (state), **Condition** (is exactly), and **Value** (GA). Click **Add to List**, click **Find Now**.

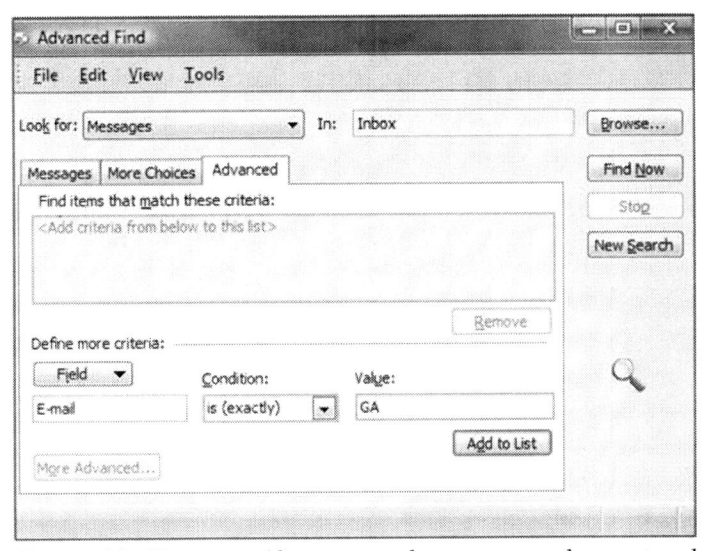

Figure 33. You can filter as much as you need to using hundreds of criteria found in Field.

3. When Outlook finishes finding the right contacts, select the first one, then **Ctrl+A** to select all of them. Next, right-click the selected contacts, click **Move to Folder, Inbox** (click **Yes** if you receive a message about how long it'll take to finish the transfer).

4. Follow Steps 2 and 3 in previous example.

📢 *If you're going to send messages to a group often, use the Define View command so you can filter contacts that meet your criteria with one click (refer to page 122).*

Send a Message to a Distribution List

Refer to information beginning on page 162 for sending messages to a distribution list (and also one addressed to undisclosed recipients).

Send Personalized Email Messages

You can send personalized email messages (or faxes) to all your contacts, a category, or any that you choose.

Mail Merge to All Contacts

Before you set up your mail merge, filter your contacts to only include the ones you have email addresses for.

1. From Contacts, go to the Navigation Pane and choose **Phone List** under Current View.

2. Click the **View** menu, **Current View, Customize Current View, Reset Current View** to clear all previous filters (reset Current View will be grayed out if there are no filters applied).

3. Click the **Filter** button, **Advanced** tab, **Field, All Contact Fields** and choose e-mail (or just type the word **e-mail** in the text box), change Condition to **is not empty**, click **Add to List**. Click **OK** until you're back to your contacts.

Now you're ready to do the mail merge.

4. Click the **Tools** menu, **Mail Merge**. Choose **All contacts in current view**.

5. Under document file, choose either **New document** if you're creating something from scratch, or choose Existing document if your document already exists. For now, choose **New document.**

6. Now under Merge options at the bottom of the dialog box, the Document type is **Form Letters**. Under Merge to, choose **E-mail** (if you're sending a fax, choose Printer), Type a subject line for your message, click **OK**.

7. Your contacts will export to Word, and Word will open. You'll then create your mail merge document as you normally would, adding desired fields (if you do not know how to create a mail merge document, refer to Word's Help or search for a video on YouTube®).

📢 *To clear all settings, go back to the Customize View dialog box and click* **Reset Current View**.

Mail Merge to a Category

Most likely, you'll want to create a mail merge for selected contacts in a category. This works almost the same as in the previous lesson. In the following example, you'll create a mail merge email message for people in a particular category. You should still filter your contacts to only include the ones you have email addresses for. You'll have to let Outlook know which category you're sending the message to.

1. From Contacts, go to the Navigation Pane and choose **Phone List** under Current View.

2. Click the **View** menu, **Current View, Customize Current View, Reset Current View** to clear all previous filters (reset Current View will be grayed out if there are no filters applied).

3. Click the **More Choices** tab and type the name of the desired category (or click Categories to find it).

4. Click the **Advanced** tab, **Field** and choose **e-mail** (or just type the word in the available box, including the hyphen). Change Condition to **is not empty** (or type it in the box), click **Add to List**. Click **OK** until you're back to your contacts.

Now you're ready to do the mail merge.

Mail Merge to Selected Contacts

You can also create a mail merge to contacts by selecting them first while holding down the Ctrl key (make sure you have all of their email addresses). You can also arrange your contacts by category and press Ctrl+A to select all of them. Everything works the same, but when you click to mail merge, you'll see **Only selected contacts** ticked in the dialog box. Proceed as in previous lessons.

Change Delivery Options

Delay Delivery of All Messages

Have you ever sent a message and the instant you clicked Send you wanted to get it back? You can retrieve the message if you're on a Microsoft Exchange Server. But this could end up being a big mess if you sent it to a group of people. You might be able to retrieve some, but not all, depending on whether the recipient has already opened it or not.

Another solution is to **Delay Send** (this is what I set up). You could create a rule that instructs Outlook to hold your messages in the Outbox for a certain length of time before it sends them. I created an exception to this rule that overrides it if I don't want to wait.

To delay delivery of all messages, follow these steps.

1. On the **Tools** menu, click **Rules and Alerts**, then click **New**.
2. Tick **Start from a blank rule**.
3. Tick **Check messages after sending**, then click **Next**.
4. Click **Next** to have this rule apply to all messages, or, to limit the messages that the rule applies to, in the *Which condition(s) do you want to check* list, choose any options you want before clicking **Next**.
5. In the *What do you want to do with the message* list, select **defer delivery by a number of minutes** (delivery can be delayed up to two hours).

6. In the *Rule Description* box, click the underlined phrase, **a number of,** and enter the number of minutes you want messages held before sending.

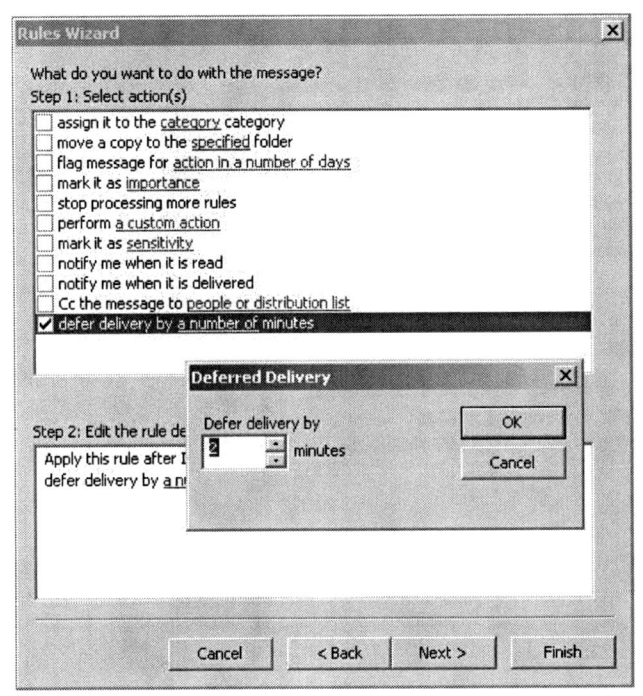

Figure 34. Always read the dialog box text. It guides you through the Wizard as you create your rules. Here, I've decided to defer delivery by two minutes from the time I click Send.

7. Click **OK**, then click **Next**.

8. Create an exception to this rule in case you need to send a message without delay. Tick **except if it is marked as importance.**

9. Set the importance level to **High,** click **Next**.

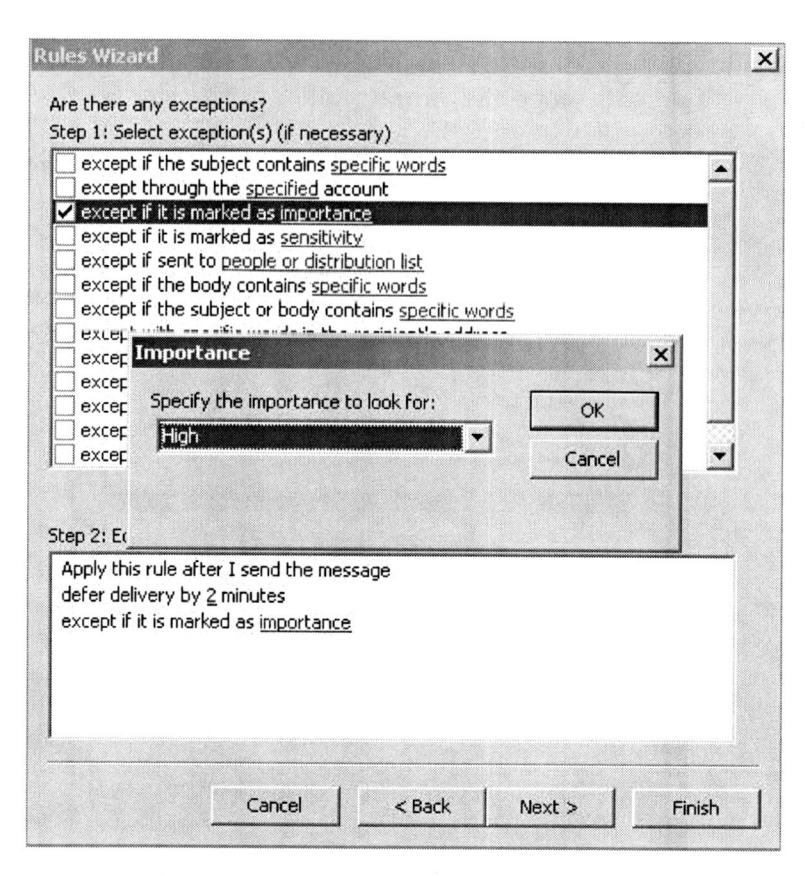

Figure 35. Here, I've created an exception to this rule. Whenever I mark a message with High importance, it will not be deferred by two minutes before being sent.

10. In the *Please specify a name for this rule* box, type a name for the rule. Click **Finish**.

To send a message without delay, create it as you normally would, but before you send it, click the **Importance: High** toolbar button.

Delay Delivery of a Single Message

You may want to create a message, but not have it delivered until later. You can set this up for a single message.

1. Create the message as you normally would. Inside the message, click the **Options Dialog Box Launcher** (arrow at bottom right of the Options group on the Ribbon). (Or click the Options tab, and in the More Options group, click Direct Replies To.)

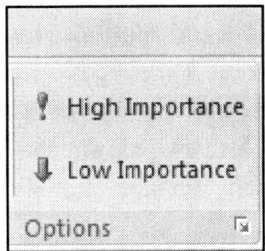

2. Change the Importance setting to **High** (if you created a rule to delay send of all your messages except when the Importance is set at High (instructions begin on page 82). Otherwise, delay won't work.

3. Under Delivery options, tick **Do not deliver before**.

4. Enter the desired delivery date and time.

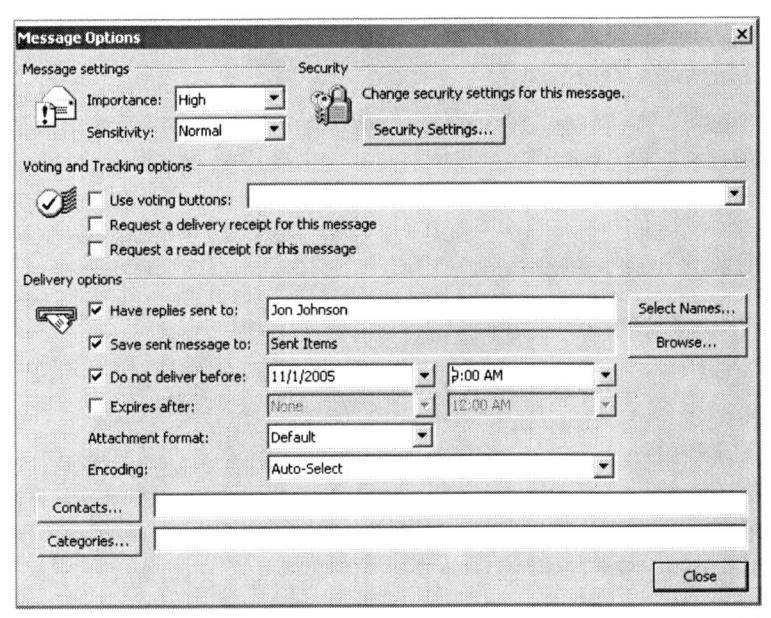

Figure 36. In the Message Options dialog box, you can delay delivery, have the message sent to someone else, and more.

|87

📣 *If you ever open a delayed message in the Outbox before it's sent, you'll need to click the Send button again.*

Direct Replies to Someone Else

You can send an email message from your address and have the replies sent to someone else. Notice in Figure 36 on page 87 that I'm also having any replies to the message sent to someone else. Jon Johnson is one of my contacts, so Outlook will automatically plug in his email address. When recipients reply to this message, they'll see Jon's name on the To line, not the original sender.

1. Create a new message as you normally would. Click the **Options** tab. In the *More Options group*, click **Direct Replies To**.

2. Type the name or email address of the person you want replies sent to, and click **Close**.

📣 *This instruction only applies to the current message. The name you entered is what the recipient will see when replying to the message. (As a courtesy, mention in your message that replies will go to someone else.)*

Flag a Message You Send

In messages you send, you can flag them for follow up for yourself, the recipient, or both. For information on how to flag outgoing messages, refer to page 42.

Insert Items into a Message

Insert Your Calendar

If you need to email someone a snapshot of your calendar, click anywhere in the body of the message, click the **Insert** tab, **Calendar**. Choose which calendar to send, the date range, and how much detail you want to show. If you choose **Full details** and click **Advance**, you can send items marked private, include attachments within calendar items, and choose between sending your daily schedule or a list of events.

Insert a Picture

You may want to promote an event or cause with an ad sent via email. You could save the ad in a graphic format such as a jpeg and insert it into an email message as a picture.

1. Create a new message, and type any desired text in the body of the message before you insert your graphic.

2. Click the **Insert** tab, **Picture**, browse to find the picture, and double-click it to insert it into the body of your message (if the Picture command is grayed out, click in the message body and try again).

You could then create a hyperlink on the graphic to jump to a Web site.

3. Click the graphic to select it, then click the **Insert** tab, **Hyperlink**.

4. **With Existing File or Web Page** selected in the Insert Hyperlink dialog box, type the URL (with http://www) in the Address box, and click **OK**.

5. Send a test message to yourself first.

📢 *A PowerPoint slide can be saved as a jpeg and inserted into a message as a picture. To promote a series of workshops I was giving, I resized a slide to resemble a postcard. I used tables, fill colors, pictures, and borders to create the ad. See www.DigitalBreakThroughs.com for classes.*

Insert Objects (Word Table, Excel Spreadsheets, Shapes)

You can insert a Word table, Excel spreadsheet, shapes, business cards, and more into the body of a message (located on the **Insert** tab).

Paste Special and Link to Original Data

You can use many Word commands within Outlook. One you should take advantage of is Paste Special with Links.

For example, you have to send some Excel data to your boss every week. You can create a template (or create a message and save it), paste the Excel spreadsheet in the body of the message as a link back to Excel. Every time you open that message or create a new one based on a template, you'll be prompted to update the linked data.

1. Open Excel and copy only the data on the spreadsheet (not the entire sheet with blank cells, etc.), or only the chart.

2. In Outlook, create a new message or a template as you normally would (for information on Outlook templates, see page 18). When you're ready to paste the Excel data, first click inside the body of the message to make sure it's active. Then, on the **Message** tab, click the **Paste** drop-down arrow (in the Clipboard group), **Paste Special, Paste Link**, choose **Microsoft Office Excel, OK**.

3. Save this message in the .msg format (see page 62) or save it as a template. Later, open it and click **Yes** to updating the link. Whatever changes you made to the data back in Excel will update in your email message.

Insert Message Into Other Items

You can insert an email message into a Contact, Calendar, or Task. Click in the body of the item, **Insert** tab, **Attach Item**, tick **Text Only** (or **Attachment**). Scroll to find what you need, and double-click it to insert.

Now that you've moved the message to where it needs to be, there is no valid reason for keeping it in the Inbox.

📢 *I do this a lot. Depending on what it is, sometimes I'll insert the message as text and also as an attachment, especially if I think I'll want to open the message later.*

Reply to Messages

Proper email etiquette suggests responding to messages within 24-48 hours. But in today's world, people want answers fast and that's too long! If you're organized, keeping your Inbox low, and you have turbo-charged Outlook as explained throughout this book, you should have no problems staying on top of email. But, unless you work for the 9-1-1 system, you don't have to be available the instant something arrives.

Consider this:

- **Do not click Reply All if all do not have a need to know.** Instead, choose Reply to send a message back to the sender only (unless everyone needs the response).

- **Do not reply to spammers.** Don't waste your time responding to spammers. All you're doing is letting them know that yours is a valid email address, which will increase the amount of junk you receive.

- **Include the previous message.** When you reply to (or forward) a message, you should include the original message so the recipient will remember what you're responding to. Click the **Tools** menu, **Options, Preferences** tab, **Email Options**. *On replies and forwards*, choose to **Include and indent original message text** for replies and forwards.

If your name appears next to your comments when you reply to a message, you can turn this feature off by unticking the **Mark my comments with** box (at the bottom of the Email Options dialog box).

- **Avoid Autoresponders.** An autoresponder is an automated email that goes out when someone sends a message to its address. They are absolutely useless in most cases: "Thank you for your email – This is an autoresponder – I will get back to you shortly. Regards." And they also respond to spammers.

- **Discourage one-word replies.** It would make me crazy if I send a message to 200 people, and 50 of them decide to send me a silly one-word message back to say "thanks"!

To discourage one-word messages, here are some simple lines of text I sometimes include with my message.

- o   No reply necessary (NRN).
- o   Please only respond if …
- o   Thanks in advance (so they're not expecting one back from me).

📣 *By default, Outlook is set to send replies in blue ink. Blue email messages are hard on the eyes. To change the default to black, click the* **Tools** *menu,* **Options,** **Mail Format** *tab,* **Stationery and Fonts.** *Under* **When replying and forwarding,** *click* **Font,** *and change color to* **Black** *or* **Auto.**

Create and Save Text You Use Often

Earlier in this book, I explained how to capture text and images you use often and reuse it in new messages or when you're replying to one. If you skipped that, now is the perfect time to get this done. It's a major time saver. (See Create Repetitive Responses beginning on page 16.)

Forward Messages

Before you click to forward a message, dig deeper. The message you're about to send may have already been emailed several times. There is no need to forward all those instances unless there are comments on each one that others need to see.

Consider deleting all the unnecessary notes and redundant forwards. Then send only one instance of the message. Otherwise, you could end up forwarding the message back to the person who sent it in the first place.

Get Rid of Carets (>> <<)

When you copy text from an email message, it may need some cleaning up before you can use it (or before you send it to someone else). For example, it may have lots of carets (>, ^) or unwanted paragraph marks at the end of each line.

Here are the steps you'd use to clean up the message.

First, get rid of all the >.

1. Press **Ctrl+H**. In the **Find what box**, type >. In the **Replace with box,** leave it blank (to replace > with nothing).

2. Click **Replace All,** then leave the Find and Replace dialog box open.

And/or you may have lots of ^.

3. Type **^** in the **Find what box** and **Replace All**, and leave the Find and Replace dialog box open.

You might also have to get rid of all the extra paragraph marks that may be at the end of each line. (These instructions will also remove the blank spaces you may now have at the beginning or end of each line in the text.)

4. Select only the text you want to change (because all your paragraph marks will be removed).

5. Repeat the steps above, but type **^p** in the **Find what box** and **Replace All**. (You're finding all paragraph marks and replacing them with nothing.)

6. Click **No** to checking the remainder of your document.

If you decide not to remove the extra paragraph marks, but need to remove the blank spaces at the beginning and/or end of each line in the text (that occurred when you removed all the >), do the following.

7. Next, select the text you pasted (or press Ctrl+A to select the entire document).

8. Press **Ctrl+E** to center the selected text, then press **Ctrl+L** to left-align it. All extra spaces will be gone.

Resend a Message

If you need to resend a message that someone swears they didn't get (or to send the same message to someone else), it's easy to resend it.

1. Find the message in your Sent Items folder and double-click it to open.

2. Click the **Message** tab, **Other Actions** command (in the Actions group), **Resend This Message, Send**.

If you need to resend the message, but to a different recipient, delete the current name and enter the new one. If you need to make a change to the message, you can (don't forget to click **Send** again).

Don't forget that you can send mail merged email messages if that would be a better solution for sending the same message to different people with slight changes.

Save Copy of Sent Messages to Different Folder

When you reply to or forward a message that has been moved out of the Inbox to a folder, you can configure Outlook to save a copy of the reply or forwarded message in the same folder as the original one.

For example, you're working on a special project and you've received related messages and saved them in a Mail folder. Later, you open the message to forward it to someone. Outlook will send a copy of that message to the Mail folder where the original is saved. There will not be a copy in the Sent folder.

To configure Outlook from Mail view, do the following.

1. Click the **Tools** menu, **Options, E-mail Options**. Under *Message handling,* **Save copies of messages in Sent Items folder** should be ticked.

2. Click **Advanced E-mail Options**. Under *Save messages,* tick **In folders other than the Inbox, save replies with original message,** and click **OK** until you're back out to the Inbox.

From now on, when you open a message that's stored in a folder and you reply or forward, that new message will be saved in this same folder instead of in your Sent folder.

You can also configure individual messages.

1. Create a new message as you normally would. Click the **Options** tab. In the More Options group click **Save Sent Item, Other Folder.**

2. Click the desired folder, change any other options, **Close,** and send the message as you normally would.

Recall a Message You Just Sent

If you're on a Microsoft Exchange Server, and the recipient uses Outlook, you can recall a message before the person reads it. But as I mentioned earlier, this could end up being a mess if you're not careful.

To recall a message after you've sent it:

1. Open your **Sent Items** folder and double-click the message you want to recall.
2. Click the **Message** tab, **Other Actions** command, **Recall This Message**. (To recall the message, tick **Delete unread copies of this message**. To replace the message with another one, tick **Delete unread copies and replace with a new message**.)
3. Tick the **Tell me if recall succeeds or fails for each recipient** check box if you want to be notified about the success of your efforts.
4. Click **OK**, type a new message, **Send**. Good luck!

📣 *A safer bet against sending a message you will regret is to never compose a message when you're angry, always fill in the To line last, read the message out loud, add the attachment first, run Spelling Check, and create my 2-minute rule explained on page 84).*

Determine What You've Done with a Message

Sometimes you can get so busy, you'll forget whether you've already replied to or forwarded a message. Icons next to your messages indicate what you've already done with them.

In your Sent folder, you'll notice an open envelope icon next to the original (read) message.

- A small arrow overlapping the envelope icon, pointing to the left, indicates you have replied to the message.

- An arrow pointing to the right indicates you forwarded the message to someone else.

You can find out the date and time of the reply of an open message by reading the InfoBar just above the From line.

Sending Large Files or Folders

Email Entire Folder

Have you ever needed to email the entire contents of a computer folder? It's easy with Windows XP or above.

1. Right-click the **Start** button, click **Explore**. Find the folder you want to email.

2. Right-click the folder, **Send To, Compressed (zipped) folder**. All of the folder's contents will be compressed into a single file (don't worry, when it's unzipped, everything will be as individual files).

3. Click **Yes** to designate **Compressed (zipped) Folders** as the application you want to handle these types of files. The folder that I zipped was a subfolder and the new .zip file ended up as the last file in the main folder. It will have the same name but with a .zip extension.

4. Email this folder as you normally would. Either from where you are now (right-click the .zip folder, **Send To, Mail Recipient**), or later as an attached file. When I've done this, the recipient has had to first save the .zip file out on their Desktop to open. They were not able to open it inside the email message.

Send Huge Files and Folders Via the Internet

Anytime I have to send huge files electronically, I use a free service at www.YouSendIt.com. You simply upload a file that's less than 2G to their server, and the recipient receives a link to download it. If you need a secure connection, they offer that too. You can also send folders with YouSendIt Express (at this writing, this service isn't free).

Voting

To find out if your co-workers want to do Chinese, Mexican, or Italian for lunch, let them vote. If you're on a Microsoft Exchange Server, you can add voting buttons to a message and process the responses as they come in.

Add Voting Buttons to a Message

This feature requires a Microsoft Exchange Server email account.

1. Create your message, clearly letting the recipients know (in the subject line and in the body of your message) that they should click the Voting buttons.

2. Click the **Options** tab and click **Use Voting Buttons**. You can choose the defaults or customize your question.

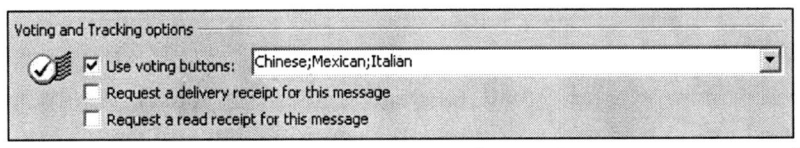

Figure 37. If you're on a Microsoft Exchange Server, you can use the Voting feature.

3. Click **Custom**. In the *Voting and Tracking options* section, tick **Use voting buttons**, then type the desired button names, deleting the default names if needed. (Separate names with semicolons, no spaces.)

4. Send your message.

Process Voting Responses

You'll have to decide how to process voting responses.

1. Click the **Tools** menu, **Options**, **E-mail Options**.

2. Click **Tracking Options**, and set processing options.

3. Save time and leave the button ticked next to **Process requests and responses on arrival**. Otherwise, you'll have to open each message so Outlook can tally it.

4. Tick the box next to **Delete blank voting and meeting responses after processing**. Outlook will delete voting responses that have no comments added to them.

If a person votes more than once, only the first vote is counted.

Tally and Sort Votes

As the originator, votes will come back to you as regular email messages. To view and tally the votes, open the original message in the Sent Items folder. (Your original email message must remain in the Sent Items folder in order for tracking to work.) On the Ribbon in the Show group, click **Tracking**. You'll see a list of totals and a list of all the responses.

📢 *You can manipulate the results more if you copy and paste the data into Excel (e.g., you could sort).*

Cast Your Vote

When you receive an email message requesting you to vote, you'll notice a highlighted line of text advising you to vote. When you click **Vote**, you will see the voting options. After you choose, a confirmation prompt will appear showing your selection and giving you the choice of sending the response or editing the response before sending.

Managing Attachments

Receiving Attachments

Open or Preview Attachments

When you receive a message with an attachment, you can right-click on the file and click **Open**. If you want to preview it in the Reading Pane, click the attachment once. If an email message has another email attached to it, you'll be able to see it. To preview a PDF, you'll need the latest version of Adobe® Reader previewer (Outlook will prompt you to get it).

📢 *By default, you'll be able to preview any Microsoft Office file by clicking on it. For third-party applications, Outlook will prompt you to search online for the appropriate previewer. More are being developed.*

Save Multiple Attachments

You can save all the attachments in a message without opening each one.

1. Without selecting any of the attachments, click the **Office** button, **Save Attachments, OK**. (If you want to de-select any of the attachments, hold down the Ctrl key and click it.)

2. Find the name of the folder you want to store the files in (or click the **Create new folder** toolbar button, give the folder a name, and click **OK**).

3. The new folder will be open, so click **OK**.

📢 *See page 62 if you need to save the attachments with the message.*

Find Messages With Attachments

If you ever need to find messages that have attachments, type this command in the Instant Search Box: hasattachments:true (see more information on the Instant Search Box on page 45). You can also sort messages by clicking the Attachment Icon in the header row (where From, Subject, Received, etc., are).

Sending Attachments

Add an Attachment to the Message

It's easy to add an attachment to an email message. From inside your message, click the **Attach File** command on the Quick Access Toolbar. Or you can click the **Insert** tab and click the **Attach File** command located inside the Include group. Find the desired document and double-click it to add it to your message.

Also from the Include group, you can insert an Outlook item such as a snapshot of your calendar, and also attach an email message (Attach Item) and your business card.

📢 *As soon as you type the word "attached" in your message, stop right then and attach the file so you won't forget.*

Resize Attached Picture Before You Send

Once a graphic file is attached to a message, you can resize it before you send it.

1. Attach a file first. In the Include group, click the **Dialog Box Launcher**. The **Attachment Options** task pane opens.

2. Click the drop-down arrow for **Picture options** and choose the desired size.

3. Tick the **Show when attaching files** box if you always want this options box to open when you add attachments (not shown in graphic). You won't "see" the resized picture. It's the resolution that you're changing.

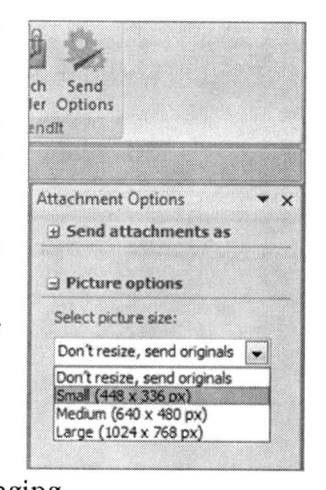

🔊 *If you're using a shared workspace, this is where you'll go to publish the file.*

Add Attachments from Your Taskbar

You can create a toolbar on your Taskbar (where your Start button is) and add documents or folders you access often. Once they're added, you will be a click away from sending an attachment or opening a folder you need easy access to.

This tip requires a three-step process. First, you'll create a new folder in your file structure called "QuickFiles" (or whatever you want to name it). Second, you'll drag files and shortcuts to folders to the QuickFiles folder. Finally, you'll create a new toolbar on your Taskbar and add the QuickFiles folder to it.

1. Right-click on the Windows **Start** button, and click **Explore**. Create a new folder (click the **File** menu, **New**, **Folder**) under the My Documents folder called **QuickFiles**.

2. Move photos and other documents you regularly open or send as email attachments to this folder (click on the file and drag it to the QuickFiles folder).

3. To add folders you access often, right-click on the folder, and drag it to the **QuickFiles** folder, release the mouse, and click **Create Shortcut Here**.

🔊 *With documents, move the actual file to the QuickFiles folder (because you cannot send a shortcut to a file as an attachment). With folders, create a shortcut to each one as opposed to moving the folder (you are not emailing a folder).*

Now add the QuickFiles folder to your Taskbar (see Figure 38).

1. Right-click anywhere on a blank space on the Taskbar (where Start is), **Toolbars**, click **New Toolbar**. Click the **+ sign** next to **My Documents** to expand the folder list, scroll to find your **QuickFiles** folder, click it to select it, then click **Select Folder** (Vista) or **OK** (XP). Your QuickFiles folder should now be on your Taskbar. (If you're on a computer network, this may not work for you. If it doesn't, ask your Help Desk why.)

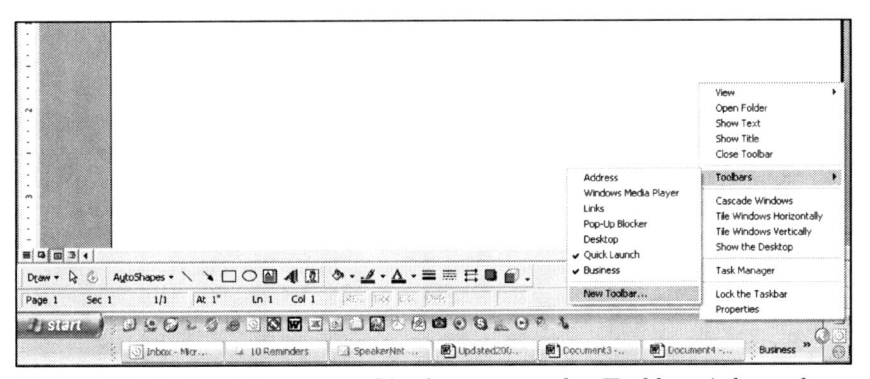

Figure 38. Right-click on any blank area on the Taskbar (where the Start button is) to create your new toolbar.

2. To access a file or folder, click **>>** next to the QuickFiles folder, that is now located on your Taskbar. Then click the file to open it.

3. To email a file in this list as an attachment, create a new message, click the **>>** next to the QuickFiles folder, click and drag the file anywhere into the body of your message, and release the mouse. The file will be added to your message as an attachment.

📣 *You will probably need to send your personal vCard often so add it to QuickFiles. From Contacts, open it and click the* **Office Button, Save As, Export to vCard file**, *and save to the folder.*

Attach a Virtual Business Card (vCard) to a Message

When you need to send a virtual business card (or distribution list) from inside of a message:

1. Click the **Insert** tab, **Attach Item** click the **Contacts** folder.

2. Click in the Items window, type the first few characters of the desired name, and double-click it when it displays to add it to your message (as an attachment). (If the name doesn't appear by typing First Name, Last Name, try the reverse.)

📣 *For other options in sending a vCard, see page 164.*

TASKS - TRACK AND REMEMBER WORK

Lurking among those hundreds or thousands of messages in your Inbox are unfinished work, demands on your time, missed deadlines, and broken promises. It's aggravating and stressful isn't it? I know. Does it make you feel guilty too? Yep. You can make all that go away by developing a system for organizing and managing your tasks, whether they come in through email or not. Outlook makes this easier with Tasks, follow up flags, the To-Do Bar, and categories.

Processing Tasks from the Inbox

Those messages that have become buried in your Inbox include phone calls you need to make, tasks you can finish quickly, small projects that require more thought and time, and major work that needs to be turned into full-blown projects. Some of these things can be done right away; others should be moved out of the Inbox and prioritized in Tasks or Calendar.

And while you're at it, get all that stuff out of your head that you need to do and add it there too or to the To-Do Bar (see Figure 4 on page 5 for details on the To-Do Bar). It'll be a big relief to see most things you need to do in one place: organized, prioritized, and systematized.

📢 CAUTION. *You should note that in the following examples, I'm dragging messages to Tasks, not to the To-Do Bar. When you drag a message to Tasks, you can delete the message from the Inbox and it'll remain in Tasks. If you drag the message to the To-Do Bar and then delete it from your Inbox, it's deleted everywhere (you'll find it in the Deleted Items folder).* **To play it safe, when you need to turn an email message into a task, always drag it to Tasks** *(it'll appear on the To-Do Bar automatically).*

Get into a meeting with your Inbox and do one of the following with each message. Don't allow any interruptions. You'll get all that time back because you'll be able to give people what they need with a faster turnaround. You'll start to notice less phone calls, knocks on the office door, unnecessary meetings, and follow-up emails.

- **Quick work.** If you can finish something in less than one minute, do it now. This could include sending an attachment someone has asked for, answering a question, accepting a meeting request, etc. And by the way, the more organized you are, the quicker you can find that file!

- **Daily tasks.** This is work you don't need any help with and can do fairly quickly. Right-click on the Follow Up Flag next to the message, and, depending on its priority, choose either **Today, Tomorrow, This Week, Next Week,** or **Custom.**

The task will automatically copy to the To-Do Bar. (You can create the default time frame for the To-Do Bar with Set Quick Click. For example, you may want tasks to go to This Week instead of Today when it's added to the To-Do Bar (see page 42).

On the To-Do Bar, it's a good idea to change the subject line so the task makes sense when you glance at it later (once the message appears on the To-Do Bar, click it to select it, wait a second and click again, then change the subject. This does not affect the subject line in the email message). If you have several related tasks, consider beginning each description with the same word. To inspire you to do the work, use an action verb when describing it (e.g., Call, Meet, Make, etc.). You can add or change details by double-clicking on the task to open it.

I use the *Type a new task* box on the To-Do Bar to jot down miscellaneous work I need to do sometime that day. If I don't get it done, it'll move to the next day.

If you're crazy busy, it's a good idea to block time on your calendar each day to handle your daily tasks.

- **Minor tasks.** This is low priority work. There is no start date, due date, nor a reminder associated with it. You'll do this in your spare time. Assign a category to the message and drag it to Tasks. (I assign this type of task to my TMinor category. I used the "T" in front of the name so I'll know at a glance that this category refers to a task. Refer to page 35 for information on creating categories. They work the same across Outlook.)

  Because this work has no due date or reminder set, you could easily forget about it. Set a recurring reminder on the calendar to review it (and update it) as often as needed.

- **Phone calls.** You never know how long a phone call will take, so don't stop to do it unless it's urgent and important. Batch these using a CALL category so you can make as many of them as possible in one sitting. Manage these calls as you would your daily tasks.

- **Simple projects.** This type of work is more involved than a simple to-do item, but it's pretty straightforward. Drag these to **Tasks** and add start and due dates. I add SP in the front of the project name so I'll know at a glance that it's a simple project (and they'll appear together in the Task window when I sort by subject in the Simple List view).

  You should list everything that needs to be done for each project so you can develop a logical process for it. You can add the steps in the notes block of the task or use Outlook Notes (described starting on page 166), and insert it into the task as an item (**Insert** tab, **Attach Item, Notes**).

- **Regular projects.** This work warrants time on your calendar and has a due date. Drag the message to **Tasks** and follow the same process mentioned for simple projects, but use a code such as RP. Also drag it to **Calendar** (in the Navigation Pane), and schedule time to work on it, allowing for enough time to beat your deadline.

If this is a major project, you'll have to devise the best system to help you stay organized and on schedule. I use project folders, checklists, templates, or binders when I'm working on something major (I don't have projects that require project management software).

- **Assignments**. You'll assign this work to someone else or ask for help from a teammate. Drag this message to **Tasks** and assign it. Flag it for follow up with a reminder so you can check the status (more on this later in the chapter).

Create a Task

When you create a task, it'll either be for work you'll do yourself or a request that you'll assign to someone else. There are several ways to create a new task for yourself. You can do any one of the following.

Create a Task from Scratch

To create a task from any folder in Outlook, hold down the **Ctrl** and **Shift** keys as you press **K** (**Ctrl+Shift+K**). If you're in Tasks, click the **New** button or press **Ctrl+N**.

Turn an Email Message Into a Task

Most of the time, when I drag an email message to Calendar or Tasks, I want to keep it in the notes block as an attachment (the email envelope) and as text. This way, I can see all the details of the task at a glance, and I'll also be able to open the original message if I need to.

1. Right-click the message, drag to **Tasks**, release the mouse and choose **Copy Here as Task with Attachment** (or Move). The email envelope will land in the notes block of the task.

Figure 39. When you right-click and drag the message, you'll see different ways to insert it into a task.

If you want the text to appear as part of the task also:

2. Click in a blank space in the notes block, and click the **Insert** tab, **Attach Item**, tick the **Insert as Text only** option, find the message in the Inbox, and double-click it.

📣 *If you don't want the email message attached to the task, choose* **Copy Here as Task with Text** *in Step 1 or just drag the message to Tasks. If you use the Move option, the message leaves the Inbox.*

Turn a Calendar Appointment into a Task

If you have something on your calendar that you want to change to a task, drag it to Tasks. Use the same methodology as described previously for turning an email message into a task.

The Task Window

Complete all the information for your task much like you would for a calendar item. You can assign categories, flag for follow up, drag the order of how they appear, and sort or group, define your own view, and create a search folder, just as you have with email messages.

Use the notes block to add any details. Either type all notes under one task or categorize several related tasks. If you choose to create several related tasks, use the same first word in the subject line so they'll line up together.

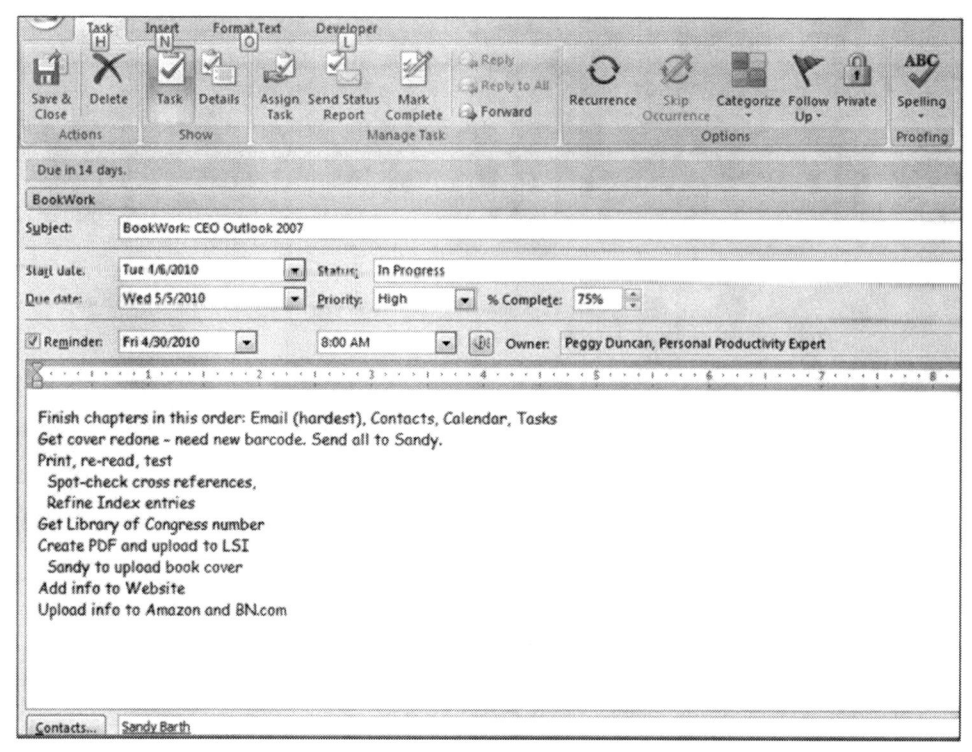

Figure 40. Use the notes block to add any details. Either type all notes under one task or categorize several related tasks. For this task, I added several mini tasks to the notes block. I also used a keyword as the first word in the subject line in case I add separate, but related, tasks later.

- **Category**. Assign a category so you can view like entries together.
- **Subject**. Describe what you have to do (or what you want someone to do). You could then keep related work together by using the same word at the beginning of each task description.
- **Due Date**. The desired completion date. (You can use words such as "tomorrow" or "next Tuesday" in this box. See more information on this tip on page 133.)
- **Status**. Continue to change this option to track your progress.
- **Start Date**. Change this date to reflect when you get started.
- **Priority**. Change this based on how important the project is.

- **% Complete.** Continue to update this based on your progress. You'll notice that once you adjust % Complete, the Status field will automatically change to In Progress. And when you change it to 100%, the Status field will change to Completed.

- **Notes block.** As you begin to think of everything you need to do to complete the work, add details in the notes block in that task's dialog box (see Figure 40). You should decide whether or not you want to create several related tasks and assign a category to each to keep them together. Or you may decide to keep all work related to one project in the body of the task.

- **Link contact.** You can link a contact to a task. In this example, I've linked Sandy to this task because she has information that I'll need. When I need to call her, I'll double-click the link to open her vCard in Outlook. (Linking is not available by default. Information on setting it up is on page 151. It works the same across Outlook.)

Add Categories to a Task

The use of categories works the same across all of Outlook, and you can prioritize and group similar tasks using them. You'll create categories the same way you created them earlier in the email chapter (refer to information beginning on page 35).

Think about the kind of categories you can create using common methods such as ABC (A for top priority, and so on). I use T1, T2, T3, with T1 being the first priority.

Change How You View Tasks

In the Navigation Pane, the default views for Tasks may be all you need. If not, you can define your own views (more information on page 122). I created the TMinor view so I can quickly view only my Minor Tasks.

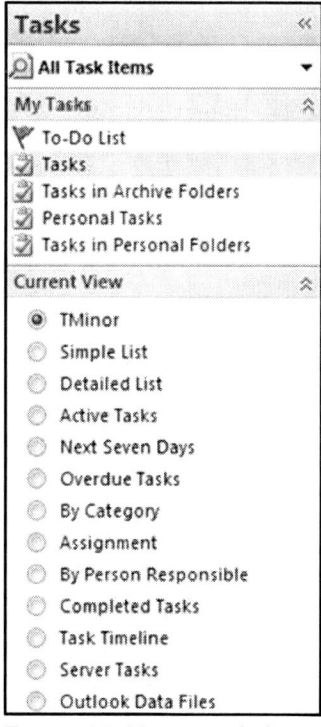

Figure 41. You can click to use any of the default views or you can create your own with Define Views.

If you find that you need to see different columns in Tasks, you can add more with the Field Chooser.

1. Tick **Tasks** in the Task Navigation Pane, under *My Tasks*.

2. Move over to the list of tasks, and right-click anywhere on the column header (next to Subject), and click **Field Chooser**.

3. Locate, drag, and drop any column to the header (see page 54 if you need more help with this).

To remove columns, click and drag them off the header.

Customize How Tasks Appear on the To-Do Bar

To help me stay focused on my upcoming tasks, I customized my To-Do Bar and hid tasks that are marked complete. (I can still see them if I need to by going to **Tasks** and clicking **Completed Tasks** in the Current View Pane.)

To hide completed tasks on the To-Do Bar:

1. Right-click the header bar (**Arranged By**), **Custom**, **Filter**, **Advanced** tab.

2. Click **Field**, point to **Frequently-used fields**, and click **Complete**. Or you can just click in the box under **Field** and type **Complete**.

3. Change Condition to **equals**, and change the Value to **No**. Click **Add to List**.

These instructions tell Outlook to only show tasks that are not complete.

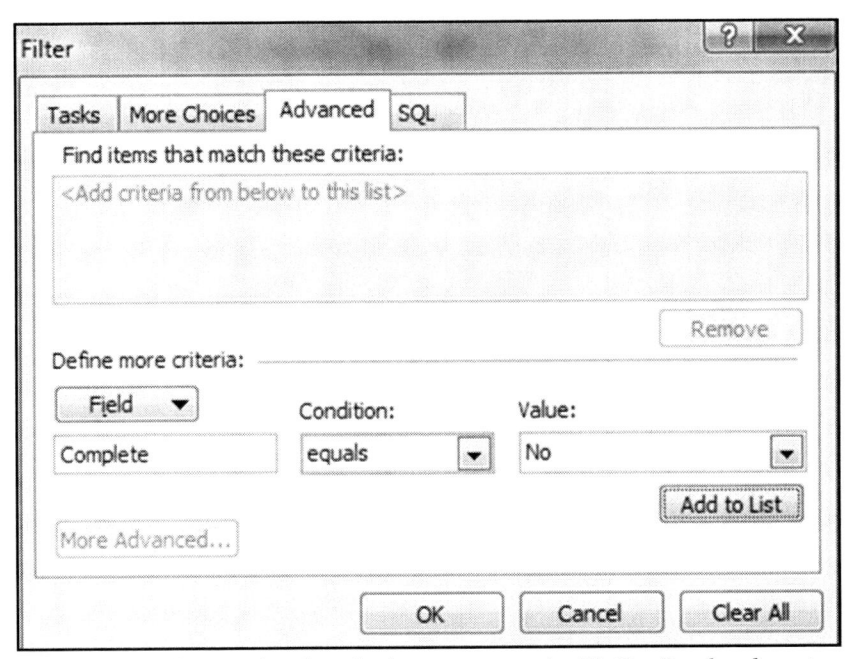

*Figure 42. Hide completed tasks from view on the To-Do Bar by changing these options: **Field**=Complete, **Condition**=equals, and **Value**=no.*

Show Only Today's Tasks on To-Do Bar

I prefer to see all of my upcoming tasks on the To-Do Bar with them separated into groups (e.g., Today, Next Week, etc. Right-click the header bar, and click **Show in Groups**). But you may want to only see today's work, as well as any overdue tasks.

You'll follow the same steps as in the previous example, but **Field**=Due Date (found under Date/Time fields), **Condition**=on or before (so you'll see tasks that are also past due), **Value**=today. If you don't want to see completed tasks, add a second criteria to hide them as described in the previous example.

Your tasks that have no due date will not appear on the To-Do Bar with this filter applied. You should set a reminder to click **Active Tasks** in the Tasks Navigation Pane so you won't forget to do the work. Or create a category for work that's low priority and establish a routine for checking it.

Create Recurring Tasks and Reminders

You can use Tasks to set up recurring reminders. What is something you need to remember to do every day, every Monday, once a month, etc.? Instead of relying on your memory, create a recurring task. Create a task as you normally would, click the **Recurrence** button and make desired changes.

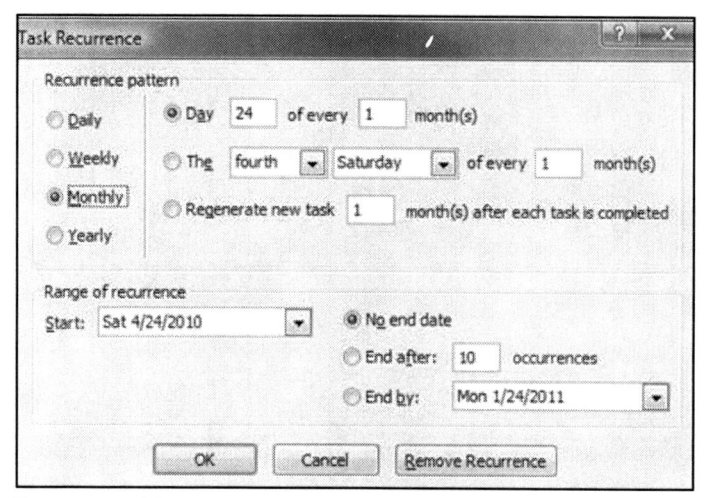

Figure 43. This recurring reminder is set to pop up on the 24th of every month with no end date for the reminder.

Stop a Recurring Task

To stop a recurring task, open it, click the **Recurrence** button, **Remove Recurrence**.

View the Task Timeline

One option under *Current View* on the Tasks Navigation Pane is Task Timeline. Tick this option when you want to view all concurrent projects for a particular time frame.

You may determine that you've loaded too much work on some days and not enough on others. You can double-click a task and adjust your schedule. You can also double-click open time slots on the timeline and create new tasks.

Closing Out a Task

When you've finished with a task, right-click on it, point to **Follow Up**, and click **Mark Complete**.

Delete Completed Tasks (or Not)

If you decide to delete all or some of your completed tasks, under *Current View* on the Tasks Navigation Pane, tick **Completed Tasks.** Press **Ctrl+A** to select all of them and delete (or hold down the Ctrl key as you click the ones to delete).

Delegate a Task (Task Request)

Create a Task Request from Scratch

You can create a task, delegate it, send it as an email message, and follow up on it later. This is known as a task request and is different from creating a task for yourself.

1. From Tasks, press **Ctrl+Shift+U** to create a new request. Complete all necessary information as previously discussed.
2. Add a category to the task if you need to (**Categorize**), and flag it for follow up (**Follow Up**).

3. Add the recipient and click **Send**. If you left the *Keep an updated copy of this task on my task list* box ticked, the request will be automatically added to Tasks (and to your To-Do Bar). You may or may not want this because every time the recipient updates this task, you'll receive a notice.

📣 *To ensure your task requests get added to Tasks, check your options. From Tasks (not from an open task), click the* **Tools** *menu,* **Options, Task Options.** *Tick the boxes next to all items, click* **OK.**

Stop or Redirect Task Updates

When you create a task request, one of the options is to *Keep an updated copy of this task on my task list*. If you leave this box ticked, every time the recipient makes a change to the task, you'll receive an update. Depending on the work, I'd untick this box and opt to only receive a status report when the task is complete. I'd also create a personal task just as a reminder about the request. Another option is to create an email rule based on the subject line of the request that would file it in a designated folder.

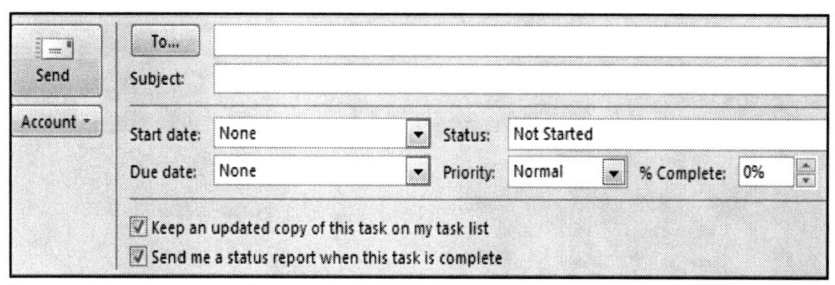

Figure 44. If you don't want to receive a message every time the recipient updates a task, untick the box to receive one, or leave it ticked and create an email rule to redirect the updates to a folder.

Send a Task Request to Multiple People

You can send a task request to multiple people, but you won't be able to keep an updated copy of the task in your task list. If this is unacceptable, create a separate task for each individual.

Attach an Email Message to a Task Request

If you need to insert an email message into a task request, you can insert it as text, as an attachment (the email envelope), or both. It will appear in the body of the request.

1. Create a task request as you normally would (**Ctrl+Shift+U**). Click the **Insert** tab, **Attach Item**, tick the **Text only** radio button located under the Cancel button. (If you'd rather insert the message envelope instead of text, tick Attachment instead of Text only. Or you can repeat the step and do both, which is what I normally do. That way, the recipient will see the text of the message and can also open the original message to follow a conversation thread, see attachments, etc.)

2. Find the message in the Inbox, and double-click it to insert it into the body of the task.

Attach a File to a Task Request

You can easily attach a file to a task request. Create the task request as you normally would, and click the **Insert** tab, **Attach File**, find it and double-click it to attach it.

Create a Task Request from Contacts

If you're in Contacts, you can drag a closed contact to Tasks in the Navigation Pane. If the contact is open, click **Assign Task** located in the Communicate group. When the request opens, click **Assign Task** in the Manage Task group.

Either way, be careful with this method because the task request opens with the contact's name on the To line, and it'll be too easy to send this before you're ready. Consider dragging the name into the body of the message and drag it back when you're ready to send. (When I compose email messages, I complete the To line last.)

Turn a Message You're Creating into a Task Request

At some point, you may be in the middle of creating a regular email message and decide you need to send it as a task request instead. I've tried different ideas, and the simplest way I've found to do this is to close and save the message, find it in the Drafts folder, and drag it to Tasks.

Another option is to flag the message for follow up for yourself and the recipient (see page 44).

Create a Task Request from a Message You Received
If you receive an email message that you need to turn into a task request, drag the closed message to Tasks, click **Assign Task** to delegate it.

Create a Task Request from Existing Task
If you decide to delegate one of your tasks, open it, click **Assign Task** (or right-click on it, Assign Task), complete it as you normally would and **Send.**

Cancel a Task Request
To cancel a task request that has already been created and sent, open it and click the **Cancel Assignment** button.

Track Tasks You Have Delegated
You can view all tasks you have assigned to others with one click. From Tasks, under *Current View* in the Navigation Pane, tick **Assignment**. Double-click any task to open it.

Reclaim a Rejected Task Assignment
In the event a recipient rejects a task you've sent, open the message and click **Return to Task List.**

Send Comments About Delegated Work
When you need to inquire about an assigned project's status, or send an additional comment about it, open the task, click **Reply**, type your comments, and click **Send**.

Receive Task Requests

Accept or Decline a Task Request
If you receive a task request via email, you can accept or decline it. To accept, open the message, click **Accept, Edit the response before sending** to add a note (or click Send the response now). Once accepted, the request is added to

Tasks automatically. If you decline, the notice goes back to the originator who could then reassign it.

📣 *If you drag a task request from your Inbox to Tasks, the request is automatically accepted, and an acceptance reply goes to the sender (this is called AutoCreate, which occurs when you drag an item into a folder of items of another type in the Navigation Pane).*

Update List
If the originator of a task request opted to receive updates, every time you change the task, they'll receive the update. To see who gets the update, open the task, click the **Details** button, and read the **Update list** (the update list includes the name of the person who originally sent the request, plus the names of everyone who received the task request, reassigned the task to someone else, or chose to keep an updated copy of the task in their Tasks list).

📣 *If the originator of this task leaves the company or the email address becomes invalid, you'll receive a deliverable error. You'll have to recreate the task as there is no way you'll be able to edit the Update List.*

Track Time Spent and More
You can add details on time spent, mileage, and other billing information to a task by clicking the **Details** button.

Send Status Report
Once you accept a task, it's easy to keep people apprised of your progress. Double-click the task to open it, click the **Send Status Report** button, and complete the message as you normally would.

📣 *If you mark a task as complete, a status report is automatically sent to the requester.*

Schedule Time for the Task
Schedule time for a task by dragging it to the Calendar or by dropping it on a date in the Date Navigator.

Calendar - Stay on Schedule

Managing your life would be easier if you get organized so you can find anything you need; set goals so you know what's important; streamline processes and stop doing useless work; and learn tips and tricks in various technologies that will help you finish work quicker.

Knowing when to schedule work also helps.

- Schedule complex projects in chunks. Complex work requires more thinking. You should stay focused and do nothing else in order to do your best work. Multi-tasking is not the answer.

- When you can, follow your biological schedule. If you're not a morning person, schedule routine tasks that don't require much thought in the morning hours and save the complex work for later.

On the other hand, if you're not a morning person but have no choice about when to get going, stop wearing yourself out at night. Turn off the television, get totally prepared for the next day, and develop a morning routine that will boost your energy level.

- Arrive at the office earlier. If your office is brimming with activity when you arrive, come in an hour earlier, or whatever time it takes for you to get there before all the action starts. Perhaps you can work at home in the morning to get important work done, then go to the office.

- Get organized for the next day. At the end of each day, put everything away, update your to do list, and check your calendar and tasks so you'll have everything you'll need for the next day. Don't wake up in the morning wondering what you'll do that day, where you're going, or how to get there.

- Schedule everything. Everything requiring your time should be on your calendar. If you have a business meeting the third Tuesday of every month, recorded in now. If you have complex work to do that will require a block of time, go ahead and schedule it too. And don't forget to schedule time with yourself, whether it's to catch up on the mail, relax, or plan your next day's activities.

- Schedule a project on your calendar just as you do a meeting. Move it off your to do list and onto your calendar!

Calendar Management

Principles of Calendar Management

Regardless of the type of calendar you use, paper or electronic, the principles of good calendar management don't change.

- **Record everything.** Anything requiring you to be there should be scheduled, whether it's a board meeting, your son's baseball game, a PTA meeting, or a neighborhood gathering.

- **Allow enough time to get to and from your destination.** Be realistic about this time, and add the extra minutes it'll take you to find a parking space, get from your car to the building, and sign in with security or a receptionist. Start from the time you need to be there and work backwards so you know what time you need to leave home and what time you need to get out of bed.

    (For example, if my flight is at 11:00AM, I know I need to be at the airport by 9:45AM. That means I need to leave home by 9:25AM. To be ready to leave home by 9:25AM, I need to get up at 8:00AM.)

- **Focus on the meeting.** Respect the person you're meeting with, and hold all calls and resist working on non-related items during the meeting.

Setting Up Your Calendar for Work

Create Text and Color Formatting

Anytime I schedule an appointment or meeting, I precede each entry with words such as EVENT, CALL, MEET, SPEAK.

CODE	DESCRIPTION
CALL	I have a phone appointment.
MEET	A meeting so I need to leave earlier.
SPEAK	I am going to present at an event.
TRAVEL	I have to travel.
FYI	For Your Information. No action needed. Calendar item is for information purposes only.
EVENT	I'm going to an event, but I'm not a presenter.
EVENT?	I'm not sure if I'll go to the event.

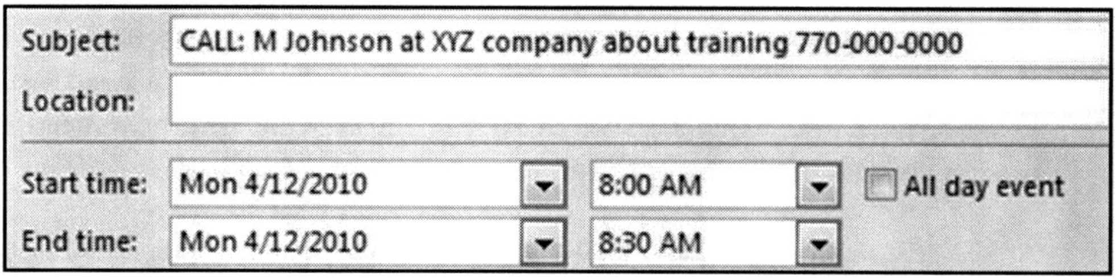

Subject:	CALL: M Johnson at XYZ company about training 770-000-0000
Location:	
Start time:	Mon 4/12/2010 — 8:00 AM — ☐ All day event
End time:	Mon 4/12/2010 — 8:30 AM

Figure 45. The first word in the appointment subject line is the word "CALL." I set Outlook up to automatically turn an appointment yellow if it has the word "CALL" in the subject line. I use a different color code for each type of appointment (see page 135 for more information on automatic formatting).

Change Calendar Views

You can change how you view your calendar, choosing Day, Week, or Month by clicking the appropriate button at the top of your calendar. You can also click to show the workweek (that you've designated in calendar options, page 127) or the full week. In Day and Week view, you'll see the times. In the Month view, the week labels show alongside the left border of the calendar.

Date Navigator

The Date Navigator is the miniature calendar located at the top of the To-Do Bar. (If you don't see it, right-click on the header, and click **Date Navigator**). Here's how it works.

- To see a full day's schedule from any folder, click the date.

- To see the schedule for consecutive days, drag your mouse across them.

- To see the schedule for non-consecutive days, hold down the **Ctrl** key and click up to 14 days.

- To change what shows (e.g., how many months), right-click on the To-Do Bar header, click **Options**, and choose.

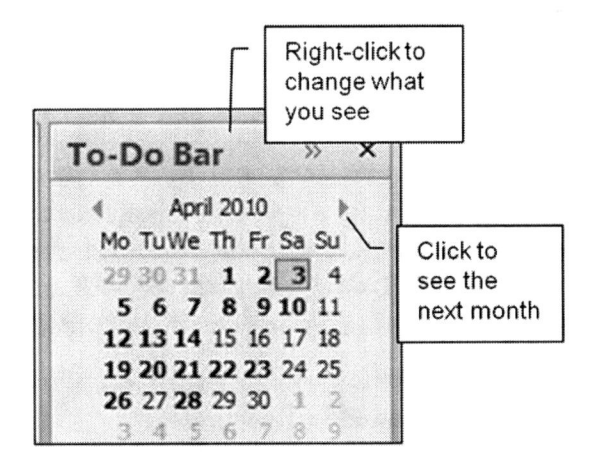

Figure 46. The Date Navigator sets at the top of the To-Do Bar. If you're dragging an email message to the calendar, you can drop it on the desired date in the Date Navigator.

🔊 *On your regular calendar, you can view various numbers of days using Alt+any number between 0 and 9. For example, Alt+6 will show you today and the next 6 days (Alt+0 will show 10 total days). To bring the regular view back, click the Day, Week, or Month button.*

For more information on finding dates on your calendar, see page 147.

Define Your Own Views

In the Navigation Pane, you can change the current view of your calendar just as you have with other Outlook items. You can also create your own views.

Figure 47. Change Calendar views. You can also create your own views.

You can view your messages, tasks, appointments, and contacts with applied filters, sorts, automatic formatting, certain fields, etc. For example, I wanted a way to quickly see all of my speaking engagements, from the first of January 2010 and beyond. Every time I schedule a speaking engagement, I add it to the Speak category. If travel is involved, I add the Travel category. The view was customized to show everything I assigned to the SPEAK and TRAVEL categories starting in January 2010 and including anything I added after that.

The following is a brief explanation of the available options you'll see when you create your own views, followed by how to do it.

- **Fields.** The Fields option represents the headers that are visible to the user. In the Outlook window, you can add more columns using Field Chooser (see Figure 28 on page 55 for an explanation).

- **Group By.** This option allows you to bundle messages into groups based on any field. Not available in Calendar.
- **Sort.** Messages can be sorted by fields by clicking on that column. Clicking the same column again will toggle the sort between ascending and descending order. (As explained on page 55, you can also sort by more than one column.) Not available in Calendar.
- **Filter.** Filtering allows you to show messages that fit a certain criteria. When you can't find messages or they seem to disappear, check the current view for any applied filters.
- **Other Settings.** You can adjust fonts and layout.
- **Automatic Formatting.** Allows you to change the appearance of messages. For example, you could make unread messages red.
- **Format Columns.** Change how the columns appear with this option, including the name of the column.

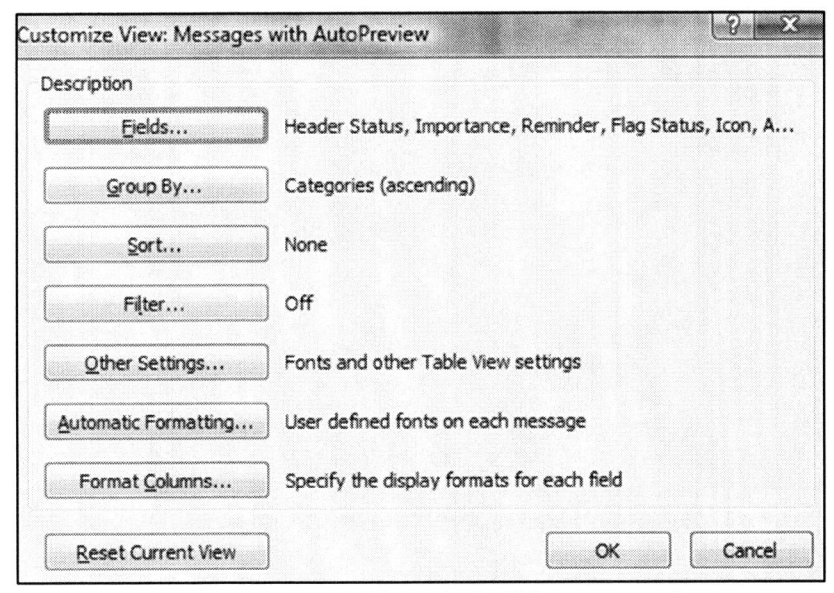

Figure 48. You can customize all Outlook folders to view them in a way that works for you. In Calendar, Group By and Sort are not available.

To define your own view, do the following.

1. From Calendar, click the **View** menu, point to **Current View, Define Views, New,** name the view (in this example, I named the view Speak), **OK**.

2. Click the **Filter** button. (If you want Outlook to search for certain words, type them in the text box, then choose where you want Outlook to look, e.g., frequently-used text fields). In my example, I didn't do this because I was only looking for certain categories.

3. Click the **More Choices** tab, type desired category(s) in the **Categories** box (or click the button to find it). In this example, I wanted to filter by the Speak and Travel categories. I added both of them, separating by comma.

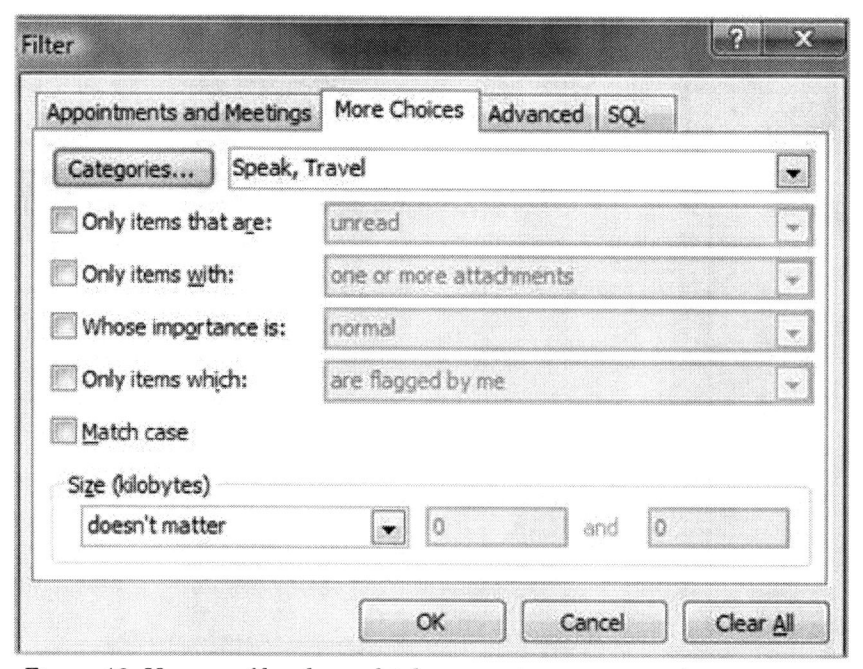

Figure 49. You can filter by multiple categories, separating by comma.

4. Click the **Advanced** tab. Click **Field,** and under *Dates/Time fields* choose **Created.** Condition is **on or after.** Type a Value (I typed January 1, 2010 because I want to see all my speaking engagements for the current year). Click **Add to list, OK** and **Close** until you're back in the calendar.

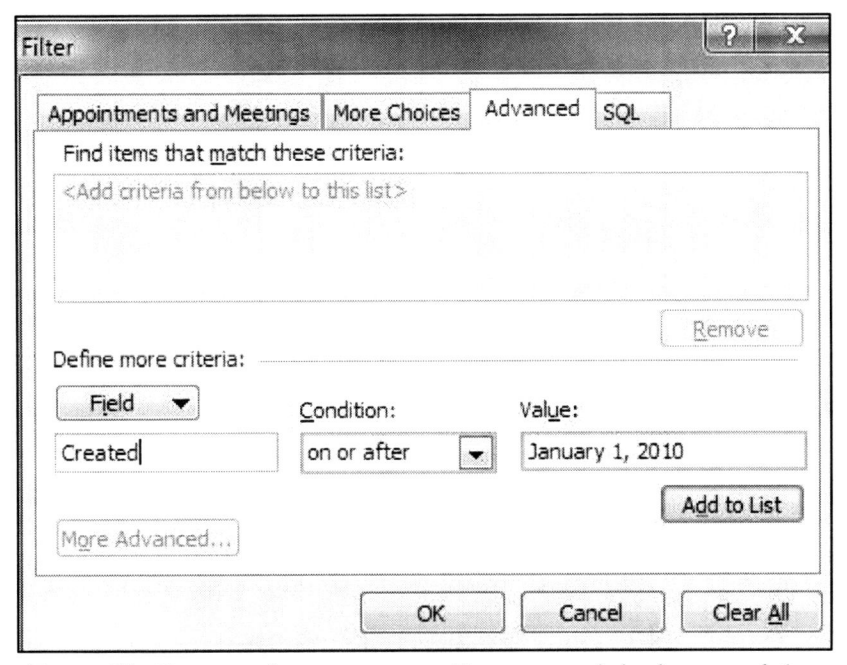

Figure 50. You can choose as many filters as needed when you define your own views. You can also add categories using fields.

When you look at the list of views in the Navigation Pane, you'll see the one you just created. Click it when you need it, and click a different view to change. (Oddly, my new views don't always appear right away.)

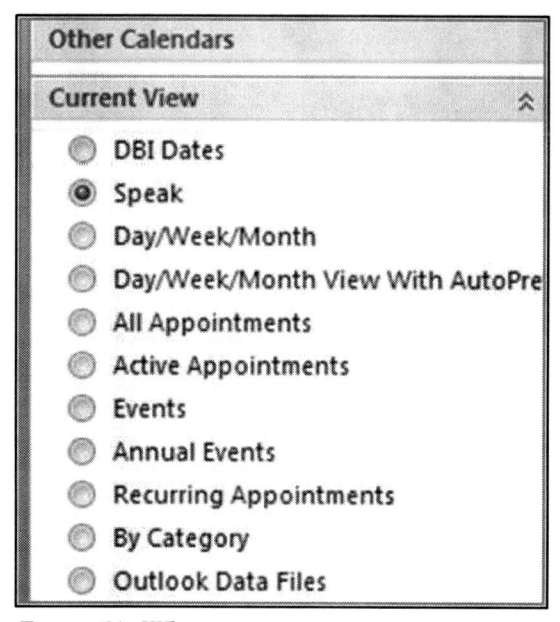

Figure 51. When you create a view, it appears on the Navigation Pane.

Use Dual Monitors and Expand Your Desktop

If you use an additional monitor, you can read email on one and check your calendar (or surf the Web, work on a Word document, etc.) on another. (For instructions on connecting an additional monitor to your computer, visit my blog at www.SUITEMinute.com and search "dual monitors.")

Once you have the additional monitor set up, right-click **Calendar**, click **Open in New Window**, and drag the calendar to the second monitor. Now you'll be able to view email on one screen and your calendar on the other.

Change Calendar Options

Mark Appointment Private

If you share your calendar with others on your network, you can hide the details of an appointment, meeting, or event by clicking the **Private** command (located in the Options group). If you print your calendar, you'll see the option to hide the details there also. Private items are marked with a lock icon.

Add Holidays

You don't have to add holidays manually. Click the **Tools** menu, **Options**, **Calendar Options, Add Holidays**.

Change Workweek

If you don't work a regular workweek (Monday-Friday), you can hide the other days. Click the **Tools** menu, **Options**, **Calendar Options**, Untick the days you don't want access to, and make other changes as needed.

Change Time Zone

Adjust Outlook's time zone to match yours. Click the **Tools** menu, **Options**, **Calendar Options, Time Zone,** name it, and choose what fits. If you want to show two time zones side-by-side, tick the **Show an additional time zone** box, name it, and choose what fits. You'll see the different time zones in the Day or Week view on your calendar.

📢 *To swap the positions of the two zones, go back and click Time Zone, Swap Time Zone.*

Change Time Scale

When you see your calendar in the Day or Week view, the time scale displays on the left in 30-minute increments. If you want to change this, right-click anywhere in the calendar body, click **Other Settings,** and make desired change.

Creating Additional Calendars

If you need additional calendars for personal appointments, media calendars, etc., from any view, click the **File** menu, point to **New**, click **New Folder**, name it, select **Calendar, OK**.

📢 *I recommend creating an additional calendar for family appointments. Put the items on your main calendar only if you have to be there.*

Viewing Additional Calendars – Calendar Overlay

If you've created an additional calendar, view it by ticking the box next to it in the Navigation Pane. Both calendars will appear side-by-side. Calendar Overlay allows you to lay one calendar on top of another. It's a great way to see a complete picture of your schedule and to identify conflicts with any personal commitments.

After you've chosen the calendars you want to view, click the **View In Overlay Mode** button located in the header tab at the top of the secondary calendar. Repeat for any additional calendars you want to overlay. To view the calendars separately, click the **View In Side-by-Side Mode** button (the same button).

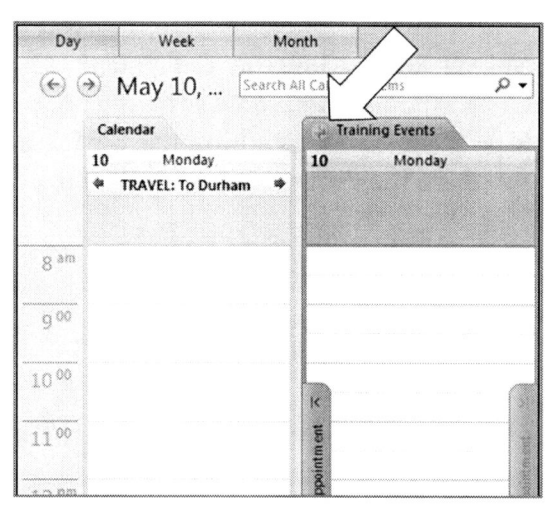

Figure 52. Click the ***View in Overlay Mode*** *button to lay one or more calendars on top of each other. Click it again to move it back. Untick the box next to the additional calendar's name in the Navigation Pane when you don't need to see it.*

The text on the additional calendar is faded. If you haven't set up automatic formatting to change the colors of certain calendar appointments (page 135), the overlay text will match the color of the calendar.

To close an additional calendar, untick the box next to it in the Navigation Pane.

📢 *To print additional calendars, click any day to activate it, and print as described below.*

Sharing Your Calendar

If you're on an Exchange Server, you can give another person access to your calendar and any other Outlook folder. For more help with this feature, refer to Outlook Help or contact your network administrator.

If you're not on Exchange, Google® makes it easy to share your calendar with anyone. Visit www.Google.com/calendar (it's free).

Send Your Calendar Via Email

If you need to send someone a snapshot of your schedule, you can do it via email.

1. Create a message as you normally would. Click inside the body of your message, and click the **Insert** tab, **Calendar**. Specify the calendar information you want to include (click the **Advanced** button for more options).

2. Send the message as you normally would.

Printing a Calendar

There is no need to use a paper calendar or planner when you use Outlook. If you want to take a paper version of your calendar on a trip or to a meeting, it's easy to print whatever you need.

📢 *My Outlook calendar is synched to my PDA. However, when I travel, I print the calendar for the days I'll be gone, including all the notes I've made in the notes block. I like having a paper backup in case my PDA dies on me and it's not convenient to boot up my laptop.*

Customize the Print Style

In addition to having an electronic copy of my calendar on my PDA, I print it when I travel (just for the days that I'll be on the road). I changed the page setup so my calendar prints the same way every time for a particular style, including the paper size, with footer text, etc.

You can add more identifiable information to your calendar in the header and/or footer, adding your contact information, Web site, etc. This is especially helpful if you decide to email your calendar to someone or in case you misplace a printed version.

To get your calendar to print the way you want, change the Page Setup.

1. From **Calendar**, click the **File** menu, **Page Setup**, choose a style, make desired changes on the **Format** and **Paper** tabs.

📢 *On the Paper tab under Page Size, you can print your Outlook calendar to fit a traditional day planner such as Day-Timer, Day Runner, and Franklin.*

2. Click the **Header/Footer** tab.
3. Click and create text for the Header and/or Footer. See your changes by clicking **Print Preview**.

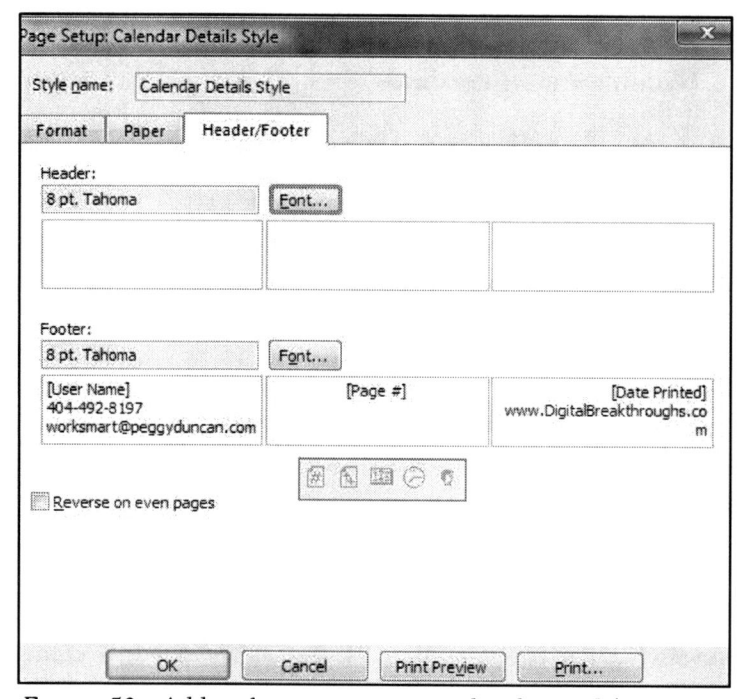

Figure 53. Add information to your header and/or footer of your calendar in case you send it to someone or misplace a printed version.

Resetting the Print Style

If you've made changes to Outlook's default print styles, you can reset them. From **Calendar,** click **File, Page Setup, Define Print Styles,** select desired style, **Reset.**

Choosing What to Print

1. From **Calendar,** click the **File** menu, **Print.**

2. In the *Print style* section of the Print dialog box, choose the desired style (choose **Calendar Details Style** when you want all the details you added in the notes block to also print).

3. Under *Print range,* choose the dates you want to print and whether you want to hide details of private appointments.

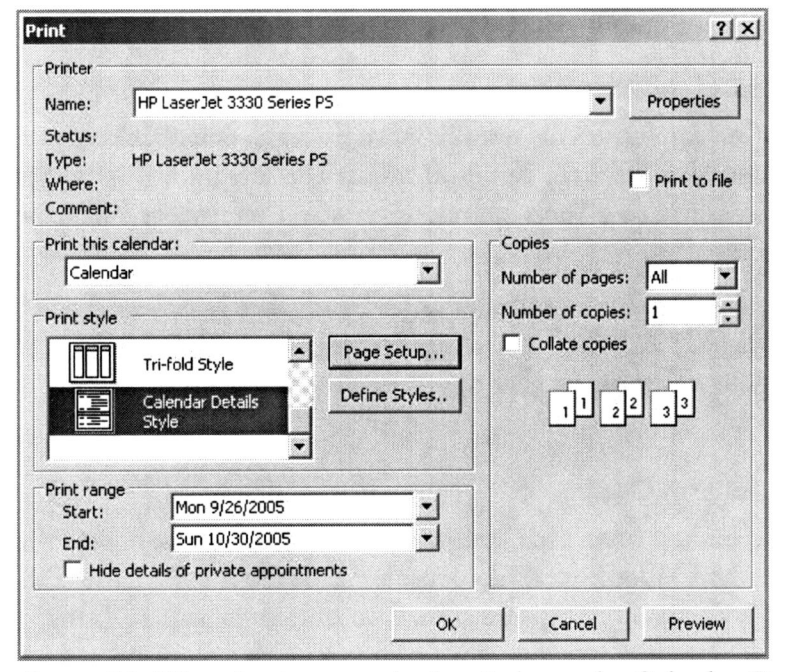

Figure 54. When I print my calendar, I choose the Calendar Details Style because I want my details in the notes block of an appointment to print. If I'm printing one day, it's the Memo Style.

| 131

4. Click **Preview** before you print to make sure you're getting what you need (if not, click Print again and make your changes).

Print a Blank Calendar

If you need to print a blank calendar for planning purposes, create a new one and print as previously discussed. From Calendar, click **New, Calendar,** give it a name (Blank Calendar works), **OK.** The new calendar will appear in My Calendars in the Navigation Pane. Tick the box next to it, click anywhere inside of it to activate it, and print as you normally would (see page 129).

Calendar Reminders

In addition to flagging messages and adding work to Tasks, you'll also have to schedule time to do the work and set a reminder on the calendar. The Outlook reminder will help declutter your mind as you try to remember deadlines, appointments, and other important dates.

Change Default Reminder

Most of my appointments require more than the default 15 minutes reminder, so I changed it to three hours. (I adjust this on individual appointments as needed.) Click the **Tools** menu, **Options, Preferences** tab, change default under *Calendar.*

You can receive a reminder as far in advance as two weeks (refer to Figure 57 on page 139). When the reminder pops up, either do the work and click **Dismiss** to delete it, or click the drop-down to change the time for the next **Snooze** and extend it.

Talking Alarm Clock

If you'd rather have each reminder pop up in its own box the way older versions of Outlook worked, consider a product called the **Talking Alarm Clock** by CinnamonSoftware.com. The only drawback to using this software is that it does not integrate with Outlook. But for critical reminders (things I'd look absolutely foolish if I forgot), I take advantage of its great interface and features. And best of all, it's a free download.

🔊 *I use my cell phone to remind me of conference calls and also for wake-up calls when I travel.*

Scheduling (Appointments, Meetings, Events)

With Outlook, you can schedule the following activities to help you schedule your busy life.

- **Appointments**. Activities that don't involve your inviting other people or resources.
- **Meetings**. Activities that will involve your inviting other people and possibly scheduling resources such as a conference room or audio visual equipment.
- **Events**. Activities that last 24 or more hours such as a tradeshow, birthday, etc.

Create an Appointment

Create an Appointment from Scratch

There are several ways to create a new appointment from scratch. Open **Calendar** and click the **New Appointment** button (or **Ctrl+N**). Complete the Subject, Location, change the date and time, change the default reminder if you need to, link a contact, add a category, make it private, and choose how it will appear on your calendar (Busy, etc.).

You can also create an appointment by double-clicking any blank space on your calendar or on a date on the Date Navigator.

Use Text in Your Outlook Date and Time Fields

When you set dates in the calendar, you can click the down arrow to select any future date. You can also type words such as tomorrow, yesterday, 30 days, next Thursday, New Year's Day, etc., to set a date. And if you want to meet in two weeks, put 2w in the Start field. Outlook will interpret the word(s) and automatically insert the correct date.

When you type the name of a holiday, this only works if the holiday falls on the same date every year (for example, New Year's Day). If you type in the name of a holiday that's already passed, Outlook will put in the date for the current year, not the date for that holiday for the next year.

When you enter times, you can skip the colon (e.g., Outlook will interpret 830am as 8:30 AM).

Add Map and Driving Directions

You can quickly find a map and driving directions for a contact within Outlook. Open the contact and click the **Map** button (in the Communicate group). Bing Maps will open automatically.

Figure 55. Find the driving directions with Bing Maps and paste them in the notes block of a contact or in the calendar for an appointment or meeting.

You can paste driving directions for an appointment or meeting in the notes block of a contact or in the calendar. If you sync this to your PDA, make it easy to see the directions while driving by increasing the font size (select the text you pasted, hold down the **Ctrl** key and press the right bracket] as much as you need to until you get the text to the right size. The left bracket [decreases the size).

Link with Contact

When you have a meeting with someone who's in Contacts, you can link them and open their business card from the calendar. (More information on linking is on page 151. Also see Figure 57 on page 139.)

Add Categories

Calendar labels from previous versions of Outlook have been replaced with categories. (Throughout this book, you've learned that categories work the same across all Outlook items and how to add them. Refer to information beginning on page 35 or refer to the Index.)

Automatic Formatting

I created formatting rules that automatically color-code an appointment based on a certain word on the subject line. For example, if I schedule a phone call, the first word on the appointment subject line is "CALL:" (I included the colon). All CALL: appointments will turn yellow. (It's optional, but this is also the color that I assigned to my CALL category for other Outlook items such as email. My MEET: automatic format matches the color for my MEET category, and so on.)

1. Decide on the formatting rules you need to set. Refer to the Code Chart in Figure 45 on page 120 for some ideas.

2. Right-click on any day, and click **Automatic Formatting**.

3. On the Automatic Formatting dialog box, click **Add**, type new name over *Untitled*, choose a **Color**.

4. Click **Condition**. On the resulting Filter dialog box, on the **Appointments and Meetings** tab, type the corresponding label name followed by an optional colon on the *search for word* box (e.g., CALL:).

5. Specify the *In field*, which is where Outlook will look for the word (in this case, the subject line).

   This set of instructions tells Outlook to look for an appointment with the word "CALL:" on the subject line. When Outlook finds it, it'll turn the appointment the appropriate label color automatically. (This is why I added the colon. I only want Outlook to make the change when my code such as CALL: or MEET: appear, not when it sees a word that begins with "meet" as in "CALL: Jerry about the meeting." This appointment will change based on the CALL: formatting, not based on the word MEETing.)

6. Click **OK**, and continue to set this up for each code.

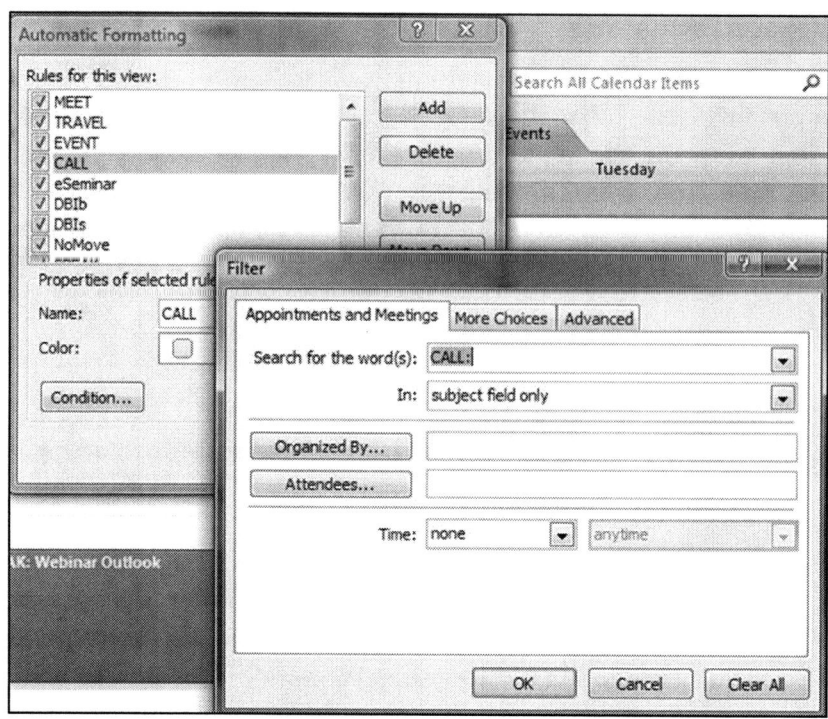

Figure 56. Use automatic formatting to systematically change the color of appointments based on a code you create and set up.

Create a Recurring Appointment

If you have an appointment or meeting that happens at the same time every week, month, etc., you can set it up in Outlook once. Create the first appearance of the appointment or meeting, click **Recurrence**, and make any needed changes.

To make changes to a recurring appointment or meeting, double-click it to open and choose **Open this occurrence** to change one date, or choose **Open the series** to make a change that will affect all of the dates (e.g., cancel it altogether).

Change Appointment Date or Time

If a meeting day changes, it's easy to make the change in Outlook. You can copy it to another day or you can move it. You can also double-click the appointment to open it, and manually change the date.

Copy Appointment to Another Day

- Click on the appointment, hold down the **Ctrl** key, and drag it to the new date in the Date Navigator (page 121).

- Or right-click on the appointment, drag it to the new date in the Date Navigator, and click **Copy**.

Move Appointment to Another Day

- Click on the appointment and drag it to the new date in the Date Navigator (page 139).

- Right-click on the appointment, drag it to the new date in the Date Navigator, and click **Move**.

- Click and drag the meeting to another day on the calendar.

Create an Appointment from the Inbox

When you receive an email message and you need to add it to your calendar, there are several ways to turn it into an appointment.

- If the information comes as a Meeting Request, you will accept, decline, propose new time, or make it tentative.

- If the message is closed, you can do one of the following.

    o Drag it to the Date Navigator and drop it onto the appropriate day. An appointment will be created with the text of the email message added. (This is usually what I do because I use a second monitor and can see my calendar/availability. To also attach the message envelope, click the **Insert** tab, **Attach Item**.)

    Or if the message has attachments, right-click and drag. Choose the option of including attachments.

- o Drag the message to the Navigation Pane and drop it onto your calendar and complete the details.
- o Right-click the message and drag it. When you release the mouse, you'll have the option of moving or copying the appointment with or without the text of the email (or with the email attached).
- o Press **Ctrl+Shift+V** to move the message to your calendar, then set the date and time. A message icon will land in the notes block of your calendar. To insert the text of the message into your calendar, click the **Insert** tab, **Attach Item,** tick the **Text only** option, locate the message and double-click it, **OK.**
- o Use Copy2Contact™ (formerly anagram), an Outlook add-in, to select the meeting information from the Reading Pane, click a hot key, and watch the information get added to your calendar on the right day and at the right time. Download a free trial at PeggyDuncan.com/anagram.htm.

- If the message is open, either click the **Move to Folder** button or press **Ctrl+Shift+V** to move it to your calendar. Complete the details.

📣 *You can always insert a message into an appointment as an attachment: click the* **Insert** *tab,* **Attach Item,** *choose the Insert as* **Attachment** *option, and double-click the message you want to insert.*

I use a combination of all these methods, depending on the situation. And once the item is on my calendar, I use the notes block at the bottom of the open appointment to keep track of everything. For example, I'll draft an agenda or add any travel details such as information from my host, airline reservations and confirmation numbers, etc. I always know exactly where everything is, it all syncs to my PDA as a backup, and I can print the details (I only print when I travel so I'll have a backup to the technology).

🔊 *I also use the notes block on a contact page to add details about the person which could include directions to his office, a note that he had surgery, promises I made during our last conversation, and so on.*

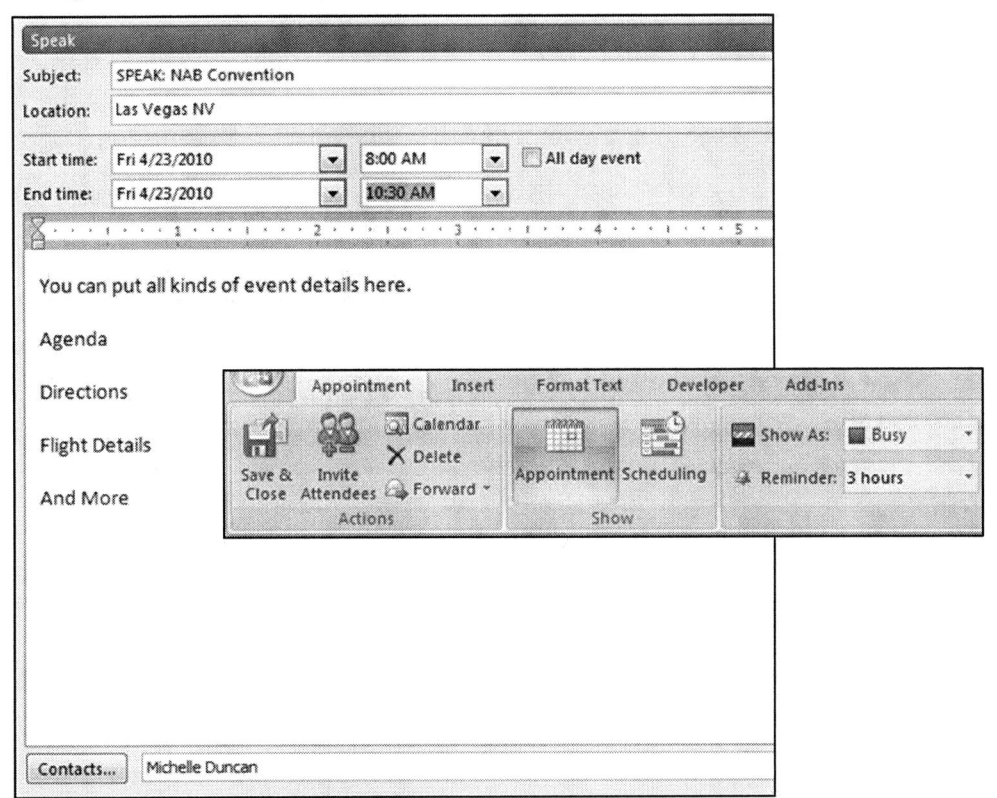

Figure 57. I keep up with meeting information in the notes block of the appointment in my calendar. Notice how I set the reminder for 3 hours instead of the default 15 minutes. If the appointment was set up using Meeting Request, I use Notes to store these details because updates to a meeting request from the organizer will wipe out anything I've added to the notes block. Notice that I linked this appointment with the contact, Michelle Duncan (bottom left. See more information on linking on page 151).

📢 *If you're creating an appointment and decide to turn it into a meeting, click* **Invite Attendees**.

Create and Send a Meeting Request

You can create a meeting request and send it as you would a regular message. The recipient(s) will accept, decline, or propose a new time. The meeting is automatically added to your calendar, and you'll be able to track responses.

Your meeting notice should include the purpose of the meeting and the expected outcome. Use the following as a guide. "The purpose of this meeting is to _____. Afterward, we should have enough information to achieve our objective of _____." If it's an event such as a seminar or conference, include enough details about it so the recipients can determine if they need to attend or not.

1. From Calendar, click the down arrow next to the **New** button, and choose **Meeting Request**.

2. Add the subject, date and time, set the reminder, add a category, link contacts, etc. (Add the recipients last to avoid sending the request before you're ready.)

    Add the location, or if you're on an Exchange Server, you can click **Rooms** to check availability.

3. By default, the current time zone setting on your computer is what Outlook will use. If you want to schedule this meeting based on a different time zone, on the **Meeting** tab, click **Time Zones** (located in the Options group), and make the change.

4. Add any files (click the **Insert** tab, **Attach File**) or other items from this group.

5. If you need to insert an email message into this meeting request, you can insert it as text and it will appear in the body. Click the **Insert** tab, **Attach Item**, tick **Text only**, find the message you want, and double-click it to add.

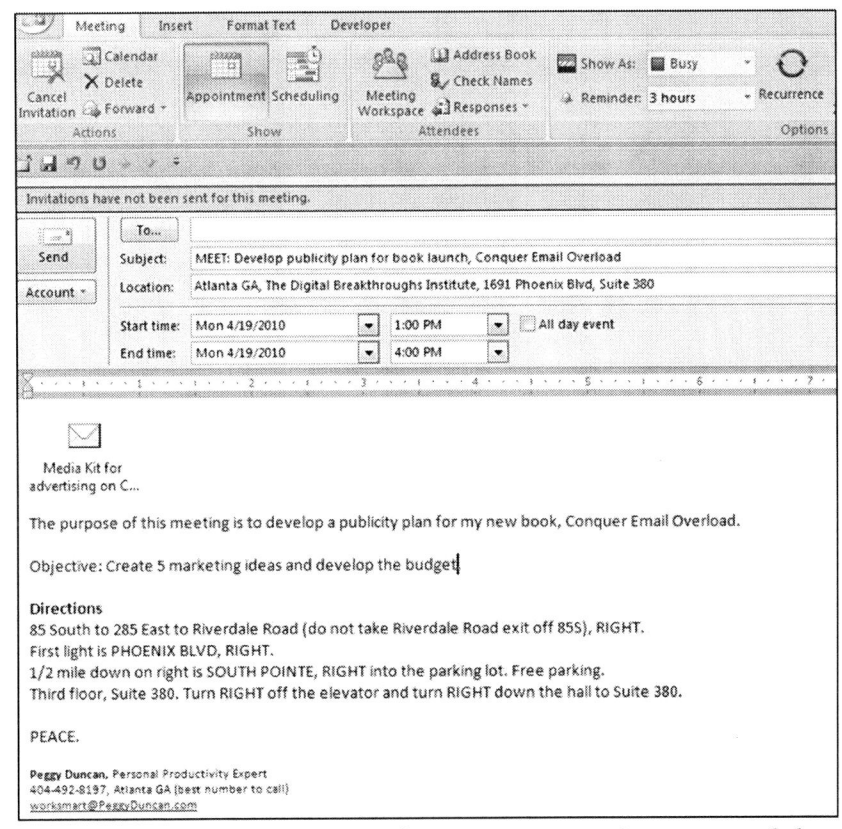

Figure 58. The meeting request will go out as an email message, and the recipient will Accept, propose another date, or Decline.

6. Click the **Scheduling** button to add the recipients, designating whether their attendance is **Required** or **Optional**. If the recipients are in Contacts, you can type their names and Outlook will find the email addresses. You can also click the **Address Book** button, add names, and also indicate if their attendance is **Required** or **Optional**.

7. If you're using Microsoft Exchange, you can view other people's calendars (based on the permission levels they have set). See more information on viewing other schedules below.

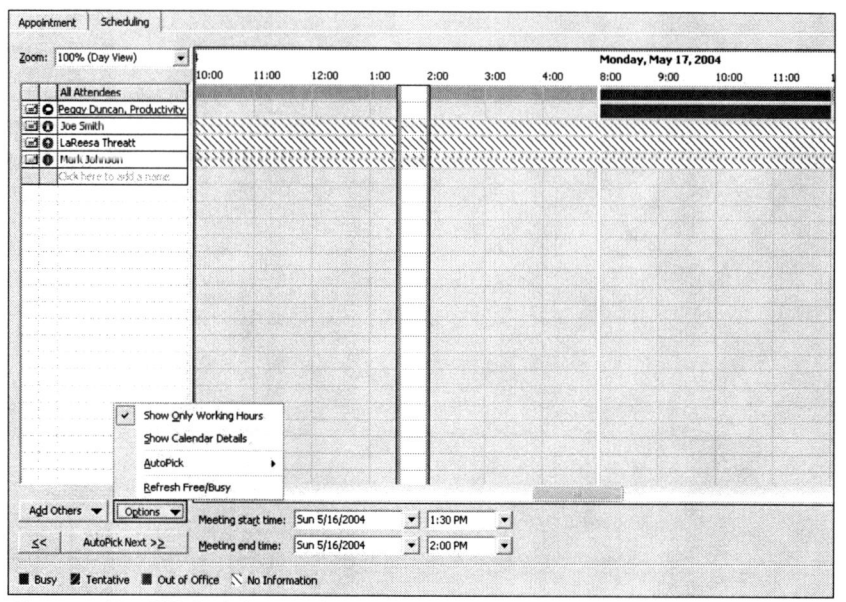

Figure 59. With Microsoft Exchange, you can access other people's calendars. Add Attendees, view their availability, and have Outlook suggest the best times for a meeting.

8. When you've finished, either click **Send** or go back to the details by clicking the **Appointment** button.

🔊 *If you're creating an appointment and decide to turn it into a meeting, click* **Invite Attendees***.*

Check Other People's Schedules

Scheduling Assistant

If you're on an Exchange 2007 Server, the Scheduling Assistant command, along with the Suggested Times Pane, can save you a lot of miserable hours calling around trying to find a time everyone can meet. Once you choose the attendees, the Scheduling Assistant will evaluate their schedules and give you a visual of their availability. From there, you can choose the best day and time for your meeting.

Here is a link to a page on my Web site with an excellent video on how to use the Scheduling Assistant:

www.DigitalBreakThroughs.com/workshops/Manage_Your_Life_with_Outlook.htm

AutoPick Next

If you're on the Exchange Server 2003 or older, you can use the AutoPick command to find a time that your invitees are available. Create a meeting as you normally would. After you add the attendees, click **AutoPick Next** and let Outlook find the best available time (refer to Figure 59, bottom left). Continue to click until an acceptable time is found.

Group Schedules

If you're on an Exchange Server, you can create a group schedule that shows you the combined schedules of people or resources at a glance. You can create and save multiple group schedules (e.g., all the people on a team or all conference rooms on your floor). While viewing a group schedule, you can schedule a meeting with or send a message to all or some of the members.

Create a Group Schedule

1. From Calendar, click the **Actions** menu, **View Group Schedules, Create a Group Schedule, New,** give it a name, **OK.**

2. Click **Add Others, Add from Address Book** (or **Add Public Folder**), select the names (or the public folders) you want to add**,** add any meeting rooms, click **OK, Save & Close.**

Use a Group Schedule

To use the group schedule later, in Calendar, click the **Actions** menu, **View Group Schedules**, select the one you want, and click **Open**.

- Send to All - To send a meeting request or an email message to all group members, click **Make Meeting, New Meeting with All** or **New Message to All.**

- Send to Some - To send a meeting request or email message to some of the members, select the ones to include, click **Make Meeting, New Meeting** (or New Mail Message).

- Send to Resources - To send a meeting request to resources (e.g., a conference room, AV equipment), click **Make Meeting, New Meeting as Resource**.

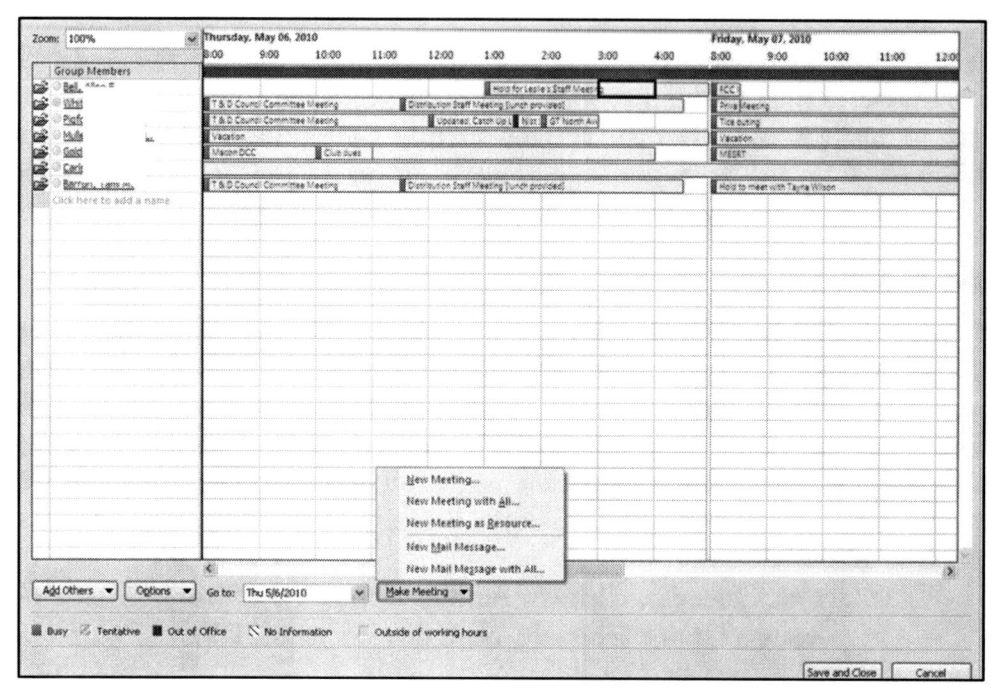

Figure 60. Create a group schedule and quickly see who will be available for the next meeting.

Schedule Resources

If you're on an Exchange Server, your network administrators have probably already set up a way to schedule meeting rooms, A/V equipment, vehicle use, etc., using Outlook. If not, refer to Help on defining a Resource Booking Assistant.

Turn Off Automatic Acceptance of Meeting Requests

If you've set Outlook up to schedule resources such as a conference room, you may want requests to be automatically accepted or declined. Click the **Tools** menu, **Options, Calendar Options, Resource Scheduling**, and tick the box, **Automatically accept meeting requests and process cancellations**. You can then choose **Automatically decline conflicting meeting requests** and/or **Automatically decline recurring meeting requests**.

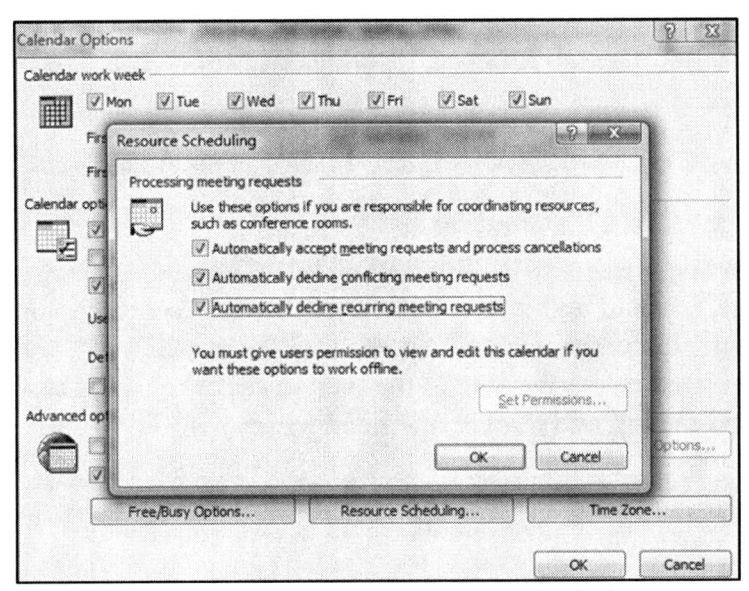

Figure 61. If you're on an Exchange server, Outlook can manage resources such as the schedule of a conference room without any human intervention.

Track Responses to Meeting Requests

As a meeting organizer, you can track responses to your request by opening the meeting and clicking **Tracking**.

To turn off *responses to meeting requests, open the meeting, click* **Responses** *(on the Meeting tab, Attendees Group), untick* **Request Responses**.

Update a Meeting Request

If you make changes to a meeting request always notify the attendees. Open the request, make your changes, click **Send Update**.

🔊 **CAUTION** *When you're on the receiving end of this update, any items you've inserted or pasted in the notes block of your meeting will be lost once you save the update. Bummer. I've started using Outlook Notes to keep information for meetings that come through like this. Right before the event, I insert the note into the calendar page as an item (**Insert** tab, **Attach Item**).*

Cancel a Meeting

If you're the meeting organizer, you can cancel a meeting. Open the meeting, click the **Actions** menu, **Cancel Meeting, Send cancellation and delete meeting**.

🔊 *If you're not the organizer, you will not see Cancel Meeting on the Actions menu.*

Send a Meeting Request to a Distribution List

You can send a meeting request to a distribution list. Create the meeting request as you normally would and type the name of the distribution list on the To line. If you don't know the name of the list, click **To**, search for it, and double-click it. If you need to delete some of the names, click the + sign next to the name to expand the list, and remove unwanted names.

🔊 *If you need to choose which attendance is required or optional, click the Scheduling tab and follow the same instructions as outlined in Create and Send a Meeting Request on page 140.*

Receiving a Meeting Request

When a meeting request lands in your Inbox, you can accept, tentatively accept, propose a new time, or decline. Always send a response either way.

- **Accept.** Offers to send a response or not and gets transferred from the Inbox to your calendar as a meeting organized by the sender. The request is then transferred to your deleted items folder. If you double-click the meeting, you can review who else was invited.

- **Tentative.** Puts the meeting on your calendar as tentative.

- **Propose New Time.** Allows you to click **Propose New Time** and send the request to the organizer for a decision.

- **Decline.** Notifies the organizer that you will not be available.

If you drag a meeting request from the Inbox to **Calendar**, the request is automatically accepted (this is called AutoCreate, which occurs when you drag an item into a folder of items of another type). An acceptance reply automatically goes to the organizer.

📣 *If you add details in the notes block of your meeting, you will lose them if the meeting organizer sends you an update to this meeting request and you accept it. My workaround is to use Notes (see page 166 for more information).*

Create an Event

An event is an activity that runs 24 hours or more such as a tradeshow or birthday. You'll schedule an event the same as an appointment or meeting, but instead of adding specific times, you'll leave the **All day event** box ticked.

Find Calendar Appointments Fast

You can quickly find items in the Outlook Calendar using the Date Navigator (see more on page 121), Instant Search Box (explained on page 45), Advanced Find (more on page 53), Define Views (on page 122), and Search Folders (on page 49).

You can also use the Go To Date command. If you need to find a single date, use the Go To Date shortcut. From either Day, Week, or Month view, press **Ctrl+G**, enter either the date, day, or month you need, and press **Enter**.

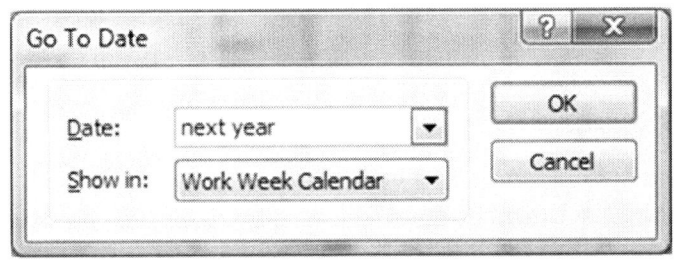

Figure 62. Use the Go To Date shortcut to find a date fast.

When you need to go back to today's date, press **Ctrl+G** again, type "today" in the **Date** box, and press **Enter** (also try combinations such as Dec, two years, next year, and so on).

Contacts - Stay Connected

You'll use Contacts to keep information on all the people you need to connect with. It integrates seamlessly throughout Outlook and easily synchs with your PDA.

📢 *If you have a lot of business cards stacked up everywhere, purge first. Consider buying a business card scanner. Trash them after scanning.*

Create Contacts – Your Outlook Database

The following explains how easy it is to build a database of important contacts in Outlook.

📢 *If you want to change how your contact names are displayed (First Name, Last Name or Last Name, First Name), click the **Tools** menu, **Options**, on the **Preferences** tab, click **Contact Options**, and choose. (This doesn't change the ones you already have. There is software that will do this, but it looks at the contact and flips the information. So if you already have names the way you want, they'll get switched too.)*

1. From Contacts, click the **New Contact** button (or press Ctrl+N).
2. Click inside each field (or tab to each field, or press Enter), and type the appropriate information. (You do not have to click Full Name or Address. Clicking inside the field and typing is quicker.) If the Check Address box opens, close it by clicking OK or Cancel. This happens when Outlook senses incomplete information.
3. Add a category (as described on page 151).
4. Link a contact with others if needed (as described on page 151).

5. Add optional details about the contact in the notes block (or click Details and add more).

6. Click the **Save and New** button as you finish each to start another. (If you need to add another contact from the same company, click the Save and New down arrow, and click **New Contact from Same Company**.) **Save & Close** when finished.

Add Multiple Phone Numbers and Addresses

You may need to add multiple addresses to a contact such as home and business. In the *Phone numbers* block, click the down arrow and choose the type of number you're adding (e.g., Business, Business 2, Home, etc.) The label names will change accordingly.

In the *Addresses* block, the default reads "Business." If that's what you want, type the address in the space provided, pressing **Enter** at the end of each line. To add a second address, click the down arrow next to Business, choose **Home**, type the address. You also have the option of adding another by choosing **Other**.

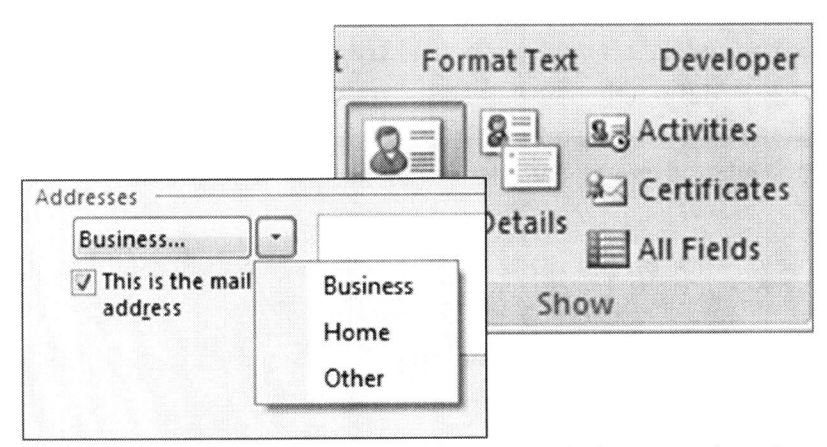

*Figure 63. You can add multiple addresses and phone numbers for a contact. Click the down arrow next to Business to add more addresses. In the Show group on the Ribbon, click **All Fields** to see more fields.*

All of these addresses will be stored in Outlook. To view them, click **All Fields** in the Show group on the Ribbon. In the *Select from* box, choose

Address Fields. To go back to the default view, click **General** (in the Show group on the Ribbon).

Add Contact Photo

You can add a photo to a contact. Open the contact, and double-click the photo placeholder. Browse to find the photo, and double-click it to insert it.

Figure 64. You can add a contact's photo if you have it saved on your computer.

Later, if you want to change the photo or remove it, right-click the photo, and click **Change** or **Remove**.

Add People to Contacts from Inside a Message

You can quickly add people who send you email messages to Contacts. If the message is closed, drag it to Contacts (from the Inbox or the Reading Pane). If you're in an open message (or viewing it in the Reading Pane), do the following:

1. Right-click on the name or email address on the From line, either from the open message or while viewing it in the Reading Pane.

2. Click **Add to Outlook Contacts.** A Contacts dialog box will open with the name and email address already filled in.

3. Complete information as appropriate, remembering to assign a category and link to a contact if needed (as described on page 151).

📣 *Copy2Contact™ software from Textual grabs information from the body of an email message, inside a document, or on a Web page and turns it into a contact or calendar item. Download a free trial at www.PeggyDuncan.com/anagram.htm.*

Linking Contacts

You can link a contact to items in Outlook (Contacts, Calendar, Tasks, Notes) and open one from the other. For example, you have an executive and her administrative assistant as two separate contacts. You can associate one contact with the other and open either one from the other (this comes in handy when you can't remember one of their names).

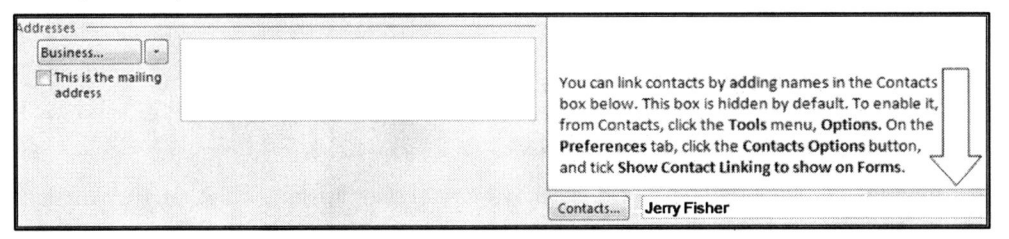

Figure 65. The Contacts text box doesn't appear by default. You can link contacts and open one from the other by double-clicking.

The Contacts linking box is hidden by default. To enable it, from Contacts, click the **Tools** menu, **Options**. On the **Preferences** tab, click the **Contacts Options** button, and tick **Show Contact Linking on all Forms**.

If you want to associate Mary with Joanna and both of them are in Contacts, open one and type the other's name in this box. When you open one, you can double-click the name in the box to open the other. You can add multiple names here, separating by comma.

Categorize Your Contacts

When you group contacts using specific criteria, you can filter your list later and send customized, personalized messages.

An example is my Client category. I can filter my contacts, pulling out just the people in that category, and create customized email messages, mailing labels, etc., using mail merge (see instructions on creating a mail merge email message (or fax) beginning on page 82).

Add Categories to New Contacts

The steps you'll take creating and adding categories to contacts work the same as they did for email because categories are unified across all of Outlook (that information begins on page 35). Just as you did with email categories, take a look at the ones that come with Outlook by default, deleting and adding as needed. Think about all the organizations you belong to, people with similar jobs, and so on.

📢 *You can add multiple categories to a contact.*

Add Categories to Current Contacts

If you have names in Contacts with no categories added, click in the *Current View Pane* (in the Navigation Pane) to see your contacts **By Category**. The contacts who have no category assigned will appear at the top. Hold down your **Ctrl** key and click on each name for a particular category. Click the **Categorize** button, and click the appropriate category.

Remove a Category from a Contact

To remove a category from a contact, open it, right-click the Category Bar just under the Ribbon, and click **Clear All Categories**.

If you have more than one category assigned to a contact, right-click the category you want to delete, and click to **Clear**.

View Contacts by Category

Once you have your categories in place, you'll be able to view your contacts in groups, either by changing the current view in the Navigation Pane, clicking the Categories column header to sort (page 55), defining your own views (page 122), or by using the Group By Box (on page 156).

Other Uses for Contacts

You can create a contact for more than just someone's name and phone number. I use Contacts to keep up with everything from my frequent flyer info for all the airlines to the serial number on my laptop.

Create a new contact as you normally would, give it a recognizable name (see my list below), and add a category. Later, you'll be able to locate the contact quickly by using the **Find a Contact** box (search address book) located on the Standard toolbar.

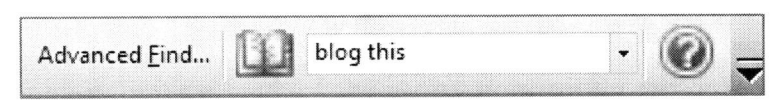

Figure 66. Create a contact for anything and find it easily using the Find a Contact box.

Here are some examples of contacts I've created, along with the category assigned to each. (When you create a contact without adding information that Outlook is expecting, a Check Full Name box will appear. Click **OK** or **Cancel** to close it.)

- **Blog This**. As you consider topics to blog about, keep a list in the notes block of this contact (Marketing category).

- **Airlines**. List your favorite airlines here, along with their phone numbers and URLs, your frequent flyer numbers, and airport codes (Vendor category). Or create a separate contact for each airline.

- **Affiliates**. List the various affiliate programs you've signed up for. Keep all the information on each one and list in alphabetical order. Or create a separate contact for each one (Vendor category).

- **Web sites visited often**. Create a contact for each Web site you visit often, and write enough of the user ID and password so you'll know immediately which one you used for this site (Vendor category).

- **Laptop**. List everything associated with your laptop such as the order number, date of purchase, service code/tag (you'll need this if you call your vendor); and warranty expiration date (also put this in your calendar as a reminder). Anytime you call your vendor, add the case number and any notes from the call, including who you talked to (Vendor category).

- **Big ticket items.** I keep all of my paper receipts organized by the month and attached to the bank statement for that month. The challenge is to find a receipt for something I purchased when I don't have a date. I created this contact and add notes about major purchases.

To keep the information organized, I pasted a Word table in the notes block. I can click directly in a cell to type, and when I need new rows or columns, right-click and add.

If it's a form you'll use regularly for different contacts, add it to Quick Parts (more information on Quick Parts is on page 16).

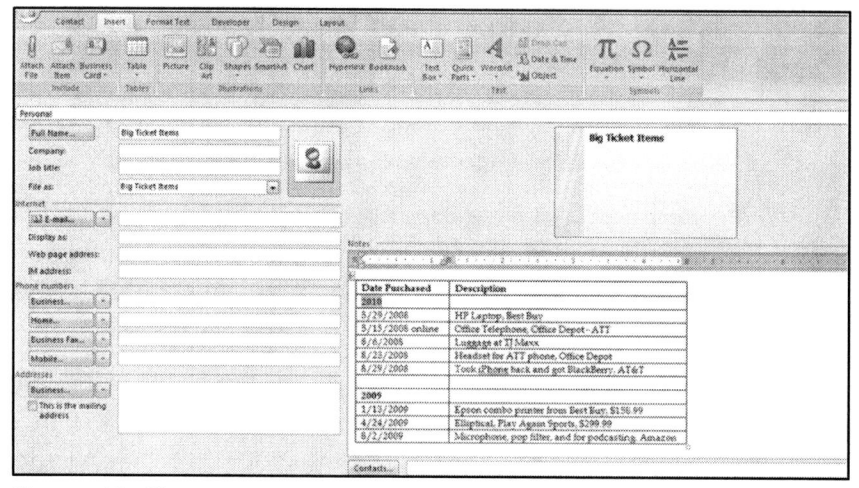

Figure 67. You can create a Word table and paste it into the notes block of a contact. Right-click to add more rows, etc.

These are just a few examples. If you have similar information you need to keep track of, consider making it one of your contacts, and it'll always be at your fingertips (and synched to your PDA).

📣 *When you type details in the notes block of a contact you can find it quickly without scrolling through it. If the contact is open, click inside the notes block, press **F4**, and type whatever you're looking for in the resulting Find box and press **Enter**. If the contact is closed, type the search terms in the Instant Search Box.*

Export All Contacts

If you ever need to export all of your contacts, click the **File** menu, **Import and Export**, **Export to a File**, **Next**, choose **Comma Separated Values** (csv) or Excel, **Next**, select the **Contacts** folder, **Next**, use the file name and path that appears or click **Browse** to change, **Next**, **Finish**.

Export Some Contacts

You might not want to export all of your contacts and will choose some of them based on certain criteria (e.g., by category, state, etc.). First, create a new Contact folder (right-click on **Contacts** in the Navigation Pane, **New Folder**, name the folder, **OK**). If you want to export a category, tick **By Category** in the Navigation Pane, click that category's header in the view window, and drag it to the folder you just created.

Another option is to click **Customize Current View** in the Navigation Pane, and change the current view with filters (page 122), select the filtered contacts, and drag them to your new folder.

Either way, you'll then follow the instructions described for exporting all contacts, choosing the new folder when prompted.

📣 *When you've finished exporting, click **Ctrl+A** to copy all the contacts in your new folder, and drag them back to the original **Contacts** folder.*

Remove Duplicates in Outlook

When you sync Outlook with a PDA, it's common to end up with duplicate contacts. There are several add-in products on the market to eliminate them, and a quick Internet search will help you find one. At this writing, I'm using www.vaita.com/ODIR.asp.

Find a Contact

The numerous options that exist to help you find items in Outlook are explored in detail beginning on page 45. The Find a Contact box makes it quick and easy to find a name you already know.

1. From any Outlook window, click inside the **Find a Contact** box (or press **F11** to move the cursor to it).

2. Type any part of the name of the person you're trying to find, and press **Enter**. (If more than one choice is displayed, double-click the one you're looking for.)

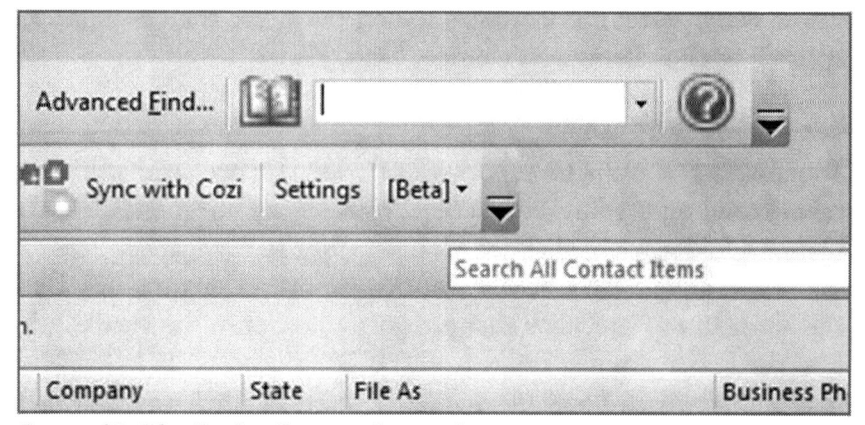

Figure 68. The Find a Contact box is always in view.

Group By Box

Before the Instant Search Box (on page 45) in Outlook 2007, I used the Group by Box command to find information such as all of my contacts in a certain state who had purchased one of my books (they all belong to my "Book" Category).

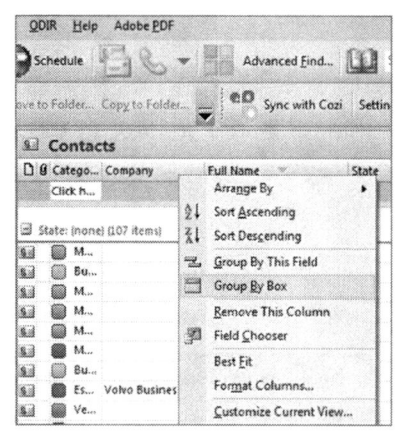

Figure 69. You can organize information across multiple columns with the Group By Box command.

1. View your contacts as a phone list (click **Phone List** in the Current View Pane).

2. Turn off all previous filters for this view: click the **View** menu, **Current View, Customize Current View, Reset Current View** (bottom left corner-if grayed out there are no filters so ignore), **OK, OK** (or click Customize Current View on the Navigation Pane).

3. Right-click anywhere on a column header. If you want to group based only on a selected field, click Group By This Field. Otherwise, choose **Group By Box** if you want to organize contacts based on multiple columns.

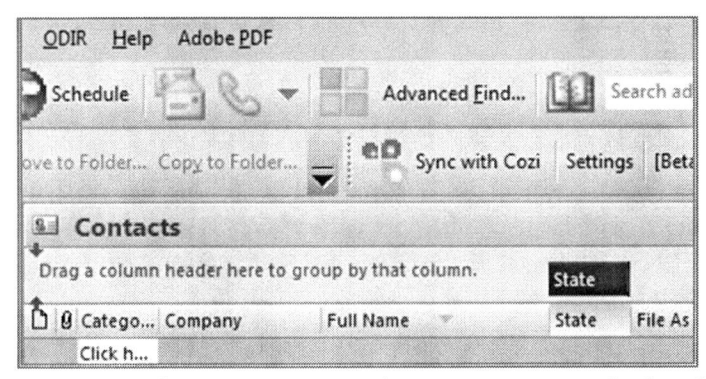

Figure 70. You can organize information across multiple columns with the Group By Box command.

4. Drag the fields of the ones you want to sort by to the well that appeared (you'll see two red arrows). In this example, I would drag both the State and Categories fields (Categories because people who purchase my books are in the Book category).

5. Click and drag the fields off when they're no longer needed.

Find a Contact Within a Message

When someone sends you an email message without a signature line that includes their contact information (one of my pet peeves), you can quickly find the phone number if it's saved in Contacts. From inside the message (either an open message or in the Reading Pane), double-click the name on the From line (or right-click the From line, and click Look Up Outlook Contact).

If you see a name in the body of a message, you can right-click on it, click Who Is, and get details in Contacts.

Add Notes to a Contact and Find Later

In an open contact, you can add more information such as a manager's name, birthday, etc. (click the **Details** command in the Show group). You can also add information to the notes block. Notes could include information from your last conversation, directions to the office, and so on.

📣 *If you need to find the contact and can't remember the name, use the Instant Search Box and search on any unique terms you may have used in the notes block.*

Flag a Contact for Follow Up

When you need to connect with someone to follow up on work, call next week, etc., flag it and forget it. From inside the contact, click **Follow Up, Add Reminder**. This reminder will show on the To-Do Bar with the person's name and also on the InfoBar inside the contact above Full Name.

When you finish the work, click **Follow Up** and **Clear Flag** (or right-click the flag on the To-Do Bar). For details on how to flag for follow up and on using the To-Do Bar, refer to information beginning on page 41.

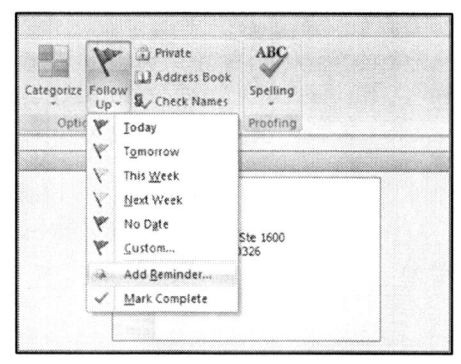

Figure 71. Flagging items for follow up works the same across Outlook. Refer to more information beginning on page 41.

🔊 **CAUTION** *It's important to note that when you flag a contact for follow up, it'll land on the To-Do Bar. Once you follow up, you'll be tempted to delete the reminder. If you do, you run the risk of deleting your contact (you'll see a warning). When you've finished with the follow up, right-click on the follow up flag, and click* **Clear Flag**. *(If you forget this and delete it, check your Deleted Items folder and drag it back to Contacts.)*

Create Distribution Lists

You can create a distribution list to send messages to a group of people at once. These people do not have to appear in Contacts. I've created a few distribution lists (e.g., media list for Atlanta), but I prefer to group my contacts by category.

Here's an example that explains why I prefer to group my contacts by categories instead of creating a distribution list with the same person on several lists. Suppose an individual appears on several of your lists and he is now deceased. You will need to delete him from every list that includes his name. If you'd added that person to each group using categories, all you'd have to do is delete him from Contacts.

Create a Distribution List from Names in Message

If you receive a message that has email addresses on the To or Cc lines, you can capture them and create a distribution list (for a legitimate use that has been approved by the sender).

1. From the email message that has the addresses you want to copy, select the email addresses (to select the messages, you might have to click on one to select it, then press **Ctrl+A** to select all of them), and press **Ctrl+C** to copy. The data you copy cannot include anything other than an email address.

2. Go to Contacts, click the **File** menu, point to **New**, click **Distribution List** (or **Ctrl+Shift+L**). In the **Name** box, give your distribution list a name you'll remember (I use the same word in front of the name of each distribution list so they stay together). Click **Select Members.**

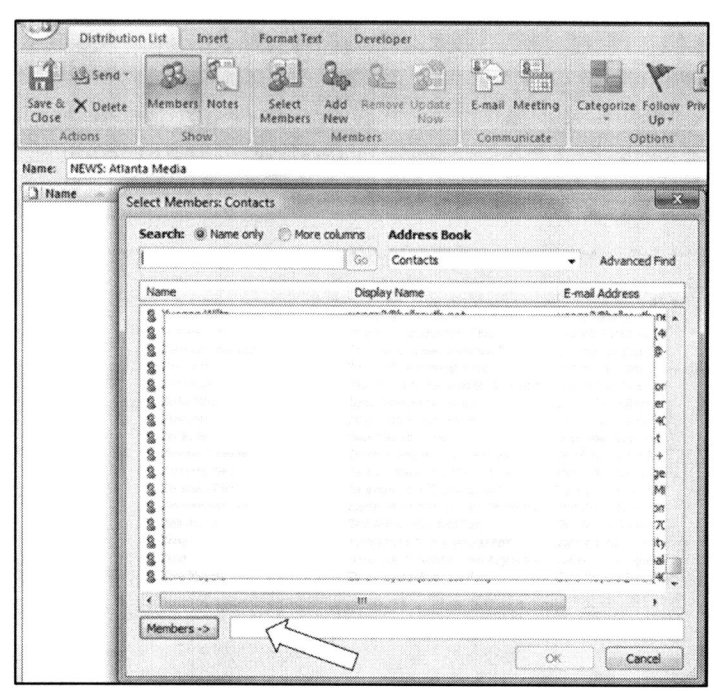

3. Right-click inside the **Members** text box, and click **Paste**.

Figure 72. You can copy email addresses and paste them into the Members box to create a distribution list. This won't work if the copied data includes information other than an email address.

4. Click **OK, Save & Close**.

🔊 *All of my distribution lists start with the same word to keep them filed together.*

Create a Distribution List from Contacts

1. From Contacts, click the **File** menu, point to **New**, click **Distribution List**.

2. In the **Name** box, give your distribution list a name you'll remember.

3. Click **Select Members**. In the search box, type the name (or first few characters) of the person you want to add to the list. When the name appears, double-click it to move it to the **Members** box (pay

attention and insert the entry that has the email address, not a fax number).

4. Continue to add desired names, then click **OK, Save & Close**. If you need to open a contact from here, double-click it.

📣 *You can also type the names of the people (or their email addresses) in the Members box as long as you separate them by semi-colons.*

Create a Distribution List from Scratch

You can create a distribution list from scratch.

1. From Contacts, click the **File** menu, point to **New**, click **Distribution List**.

2. In the **Name** box, give your distribution list a name you'll remember, then click the **Add New** command.

3. In the **Add New Member** box, type the person's name and email address. Repeat until you're finished.

📣 *All of my distribution lists start with the same word to keep them filed together.*

Update a Distribution List

To update information in a distribution list, find the list by typing part of the name in the Find a Contact box (see page 155) and pressing **Enter**. Double-click the list name, and make desired changes. To delete someone, click the name, then click the **Remove** button (not the Delete toolbar button. If you use the X Delete toolbar button, you'll delete your entire list. You'll be able to retrieve it from your Deleted Items folder).

Remove a Name from a Distribution List

It's easy to delete the entire distribution list when all you wanted to do is to delete a name. That's because the Delete button, the big **X**, is so prominently displayed. When you need to remove a name for a list, select it and click **Remove**.

📣 *If you accidentally delete your distribution list, you'll find it in the Deleted Items folder. Drag it back to Contacts.*

Find a Distribution List

When I'm looking for a distribution list and I'm not sure of the one I need, I click the Address Book icon (see Figure 74 on page 164) instead of typing inside the Find a Contact box. The difference is that the Address Book stays open after you double-click a list to open it. If you've opened the wrong list, you can slide back to the Address Book.

📢 *You'll appreciate starting all lists with the same word when you have to find one.*

Send a Message to a Distribution List

Once your distribution list is created, you can send a message to everyone on it just as you do to an individual.

1. From the Inbox, create a new email message. Complete the message before you add the names (just a precaution against clicking to send before you're ready).

2. Click the **Bcc** button, click in the search box to find your list, double-click it, click **OK**.

📢 *If you want to review the list before you insert it, right-click it and click* **Properties**. *To continue, press* **Esc**, *then double-click it to insert. Use Bcc to protect the privacy of the names in your list.*

If the distribution list is already open, click **E-mail** in the Communicate group. When the message opens, move the list to the Bcc box.

Expand Distribution List and Delete Names

When you add a distribution list to the To, Cc, or Bcc boxes of your email message, the Expand List command (a plus sign) appears to the left of the list name. Click it to expand the list so you can delete any names you may not want to send the message to (deleting names only applies to this message).

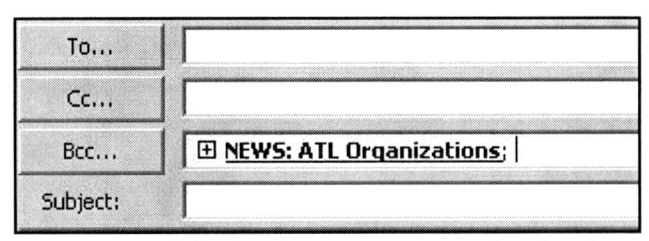

Figure 73. Click the plus sign next to the distribution list name to expand the list.

Send Email Addressed to Undisclosed Recipients

If you've seen an email addressed to Undisclosed Recipients and wondered how it was done, here are two options.

- **First Option**. When you create a new message, type Undisclosed Recipients on the To line, and next to that put your email address inside brackets < >. Then refer to the second option to finish the message. (The recipient of your message, will only see Undisclosed Recipients on the To line, not your email address.)

- **Second Option** (this is what I've done so I don't have to remember anything later).

   Create a new Outlook contact:

1. **Full Name**: Undisclosed Recipients.
2. **E-mail**: Add whatever address you'll send the email from.
3. **Display as**: Undisclosed Recipients.
4. When you **Save & Close** the new contact, if you get a message indicating duplication, choose **Add this contact anyway**. This message appears because you probably used the same email address on your contact page (if you created one).

When you create your message, type **Undisclosed Recipients** on the **To** line. When you're ready to send, put the email addresses (or a distribution list name) on the **Bcc** line, and send the message as you normally would. (If you don't see Bcc, click the **Options** tab, **Show Bcc**.)

🔊 *Finish the message before you add the recipient names (so you won't send the email before you're ready). Recipients will only see their email address when you use Bcc, even if they click Reply to All.*

Send a vCard or Distribution List

If a contact you need to send is already open, click **Send** (located in the Actions group), **In Internet Format (vCard)** to create a new message with the vCard attached. You can also right-click on a contact from any view, point to **Send Full Contact**, and click **In Internet Format (vCard)**.

(If you're inside of a message and need to attach a vCard, click the **Insert** tab, **Attach Item, Contacts**, find it, double-click it to attach to the message.)

🔊 *If you receive a vCard from someone, drag it to Contacts.*

Send Distribution List to Another User

You can send a distribution list to another user by emailing it.

1. From Contacts, press **F11** to send your cursor to the **Find a Contact** box (search address book).

2. Type the distribution list (or contact) name (or part of it) in the Find a Contact box, and press **Enter**. (If you typed part of the name, the Choose Contact dialog box will open.)

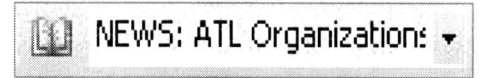

Figure 74. You can type part of the distribution name to find it. (FYI, in this figure, that's the Address Book icon on the left.)

3. Double-click the desired list to open it (if you typed part of the name).

4. Click **Send** (in the Actions group), **In Internet Format (vCard)**. Finish your message and send it as you normally would.

Save a Distribution List or vCard You Receive

When you receive a vCard or distribution list in email, drag it from the Inbox Reading Pane and drop it onto the **Contacts** folder or icon in the Navigation Pane.

Move a Distribution List to a New Computer

Distribution lists do not export well. The simplest way to move a list to another computer is to email the file to yourself and receive it on the new computer.

Print a Distribution List

You can print your distribution list if you ever need to. Double-click the list to open it, click the **Office** button, **Print,** and print it as you would any document.

Notes – Use to Remember

Outlook includes the equivalent of electronic sticky notes. If you're accustomed to leaving paper notes all over your computer, these could take their place. Once you devise a way to use Notes and get into the habit of using them, they'll become quite handy.

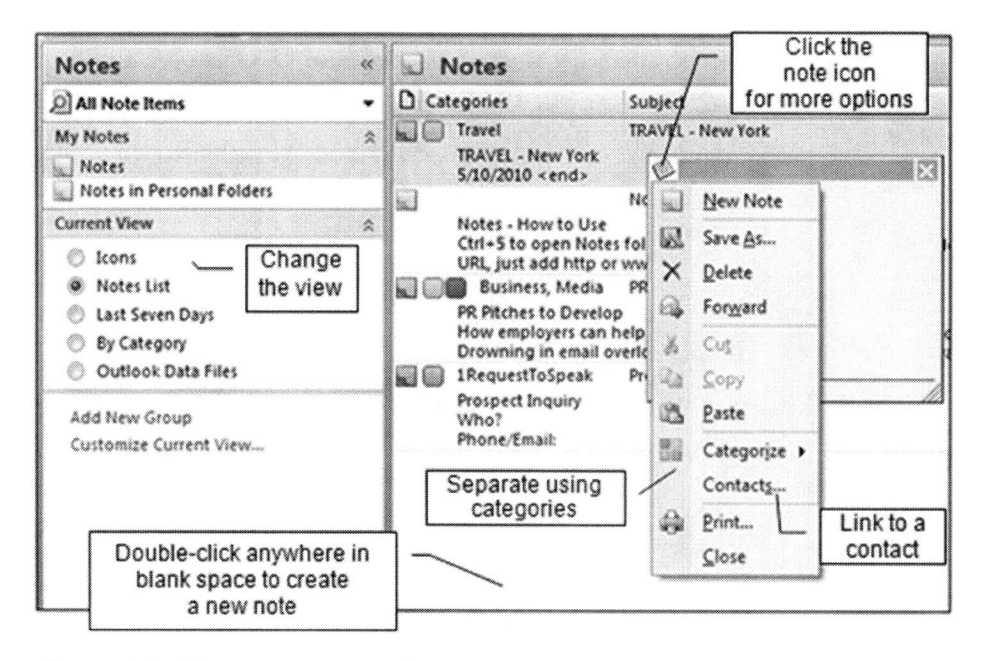

Figure 75. Electronic notes make it easier and neater to keep up with bits of information.

📢 In the chapter on calendaring, I mentioned how updates to meeting requests wipe out any notes you may have added in the notes block. When I discovered that the hard way, I started using Notes for travel details, directions, agenda items, etc. At some point, I'll insert the note into the calendar as text. The best thing about this is that if the organizer sends another meeting update, my text is still in the original note.

Create a Note

The following are steps that will help you get started with Outlook Notes.

*Figure 76. The electronic note is the perfect place for tidbits of information you're keeping everywhere. For more options, click the notes icon in upper left corner. To copy a note, tick **Icons** under Current View (in Navigation Pane), click the note you want to copy, hold down **Ctrl** and drag. The Date/Time at the bottom of the note reflects the last edit, not the create date.*

1. Press **Ctrl+5** to open the Notes folder. Double-click anywhere in a blank space to create a new note. Create the title with the first line you type (Outlook saves the note as soon as you start typing). You can also save the note outside the Notes folder by clicking the **Note** icon, **Save As**.

2. Add a URL by typing it as you normally would with http or www.

3. Click the **Note icon** for more options such as Print, etc.

4. Link the note to a contact. Click the **Note** icon, **Contacts, Contacts** button to browse. Later, you can see the notes for that contact. Open the contact, click **Activities**, click the down arrow next to **Show**, and choose **Notes**.

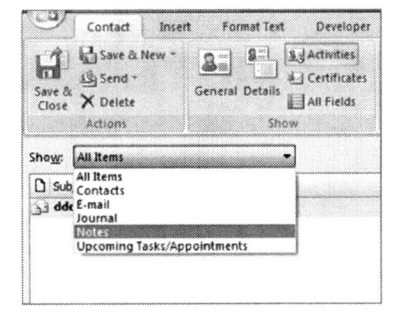

You can create a filing system for Notes just as you have for the Inbox: right-click the **Notes** folder, **New Folder**. You can also customize how you view Notes the same as you've done for other Outlook items.

MAINTENANCE

Now that you're using Outlook to manage your whole life, you'll have to keep it running smoothly and completely backed up.

Archive

You can archive old Outlook files after a certain number of days, either automatically (AutoArchive) or manually. The following is a list of the folders that have the AutoArchive feature turned on with their default aging period. There is no AutoArchive feature for Contacts.

- Calendar (6 months).
- Messages - Sent Items (2 months).
- Messages - Deleted Items (2 months).
- Tasks (6 months).

I changed my Sent folder to AutoArchive every three months. Then once a year, I decide what to delete from the archives.

1. Right-click on the **Sent Items** folder, click **Properties**.
2. Click the **AutoArchive** tab, tick desired settings (under *Archive this folder using these settings* and under *Clean out items older than*, I chose **3 Months**. Also ticked is **Move old items to default archive folder**.

📢 *If you have any special configuration such as synching your laptop to a PC, your capabilities might be different (e.g., you might only be able to archive files on the PC). Archiving items does not change the message format.*

AutoArchive Instead of Deleting

I'm real big on deleting. Real big. My Deleted Items folder needs to be cleaned out often. Instead of having Outlook empty it automatically when I exit (might need something), I set it up to AutoArchive every three weeks and permanently delete older messages.

Archive Files Manually

AutoArchive means set it and forget it, but if for some reason you want to archive your files manually, it's easy. You can autoarchive all of your Outlook folders except Contacts. Click the **File** menu, **Archive**, choose desired folder, enter "older than" date, **Browse** to change the file location if needed, **OK**.

Find Archived Files

The Archive folder is at the bottom of your Folder List in the Navigation Pane. If you don't see one, click the **Tools** menu, **Options**, **Other** tab, **AutoArchive**, and tick the box labelled *Show archive folder in folder list*. If this box is greyed out, you'll need to set up AutoArchiving as previously described. To open an archived folder, double-click it.

Back Up Your Data

A backup is not a backup if it's not off site or if you only have one version of a file. I'm amazed when I hear people say they back up their files on a flash drive, CD, etc. What's amazing is that what they are actually doing is saving the files, not backing up a copy of the files. And for those of you who are actually saving a copy of a file, where are you keeping the medium they're stored on? If it's in the same place as your computer, it's not a backup.

    Don't lose all your hard work. Schedule a reminder in Outlook to back up important data. Then save that backup somewhere else. To back up your files, use an external hard drive (that's set to do it automatically) or whatever works for you.

    My files are backed up online automatically several times a day. Visit my Web site for more details at www.PeggyDuncan.com/mozypro.htm.

Check Folder Sizes

If you need to know how much storage space any of the files in Outlook are, click the **Tools** menu, **Mailbox Cleanup**, **View Mailbox Size**. The sizes are measured in KB (1,000 bytes=approximately 1 KB; 1,000 KB=approximately 1 MB; 1,000 MB=approximately 1 GB).

Back Up (Almost) Everything at Once (.pst)

Outlook data is saved in the .pst format. A .pst file is stored locally on your hard drive. It's a portable file that can be moved from one computer to another, but you'll need Outlook to use it. You can back up messages, contacts, appointments, tasks, notes, journal entries, and rules (all saved in the .pst file).

Microsoft offers a free tool that makes it easy to backup your .pst file. For more information, visit www.PeggyDuncan.com/downloads.htm.

You can also back up manually.

1. Get an external storage device ready to store a large file (flash drive, CD, etc.). A flash drive is better because if you burn to a CD, the file will become Read Only. (To use it, you'll have to right-click on it, click Properties, and untick Read-only.)

2. In Outlook, click the **File** menu, **Data File Management**.

3. Click **Personal Folders, Open Folder** button.

4. Close Outlook after .pst files appear.

5. Right-click the **Outlook.pst** file, **Send To**, choose drive you set up in Step 1.

   If you get an error message about another process having Outlook locked, shut down other applications such as MSN Desktop Search, Yahoo! or Google Desktop Search, etc. You should also uncradle your PDA and disable all Outlook add-ins. Finally, press **Ctrl+Alt+Delete**, click **Start Task Manager**, and close anything Outlook-related.

📣 *You can only open a .pst file from within Outlook. I've read that if it gets larger than 2GB, it could stop functioning. My .pst file is backed up online with MozyPro (see www.PeggyDuncan.com/mozypro.htm).*

Back Up Your Rules

Rules are now part of the .pst file and will be backed up with it. If you'd like to also back them up separately, here's how.

1. From Mail, click the **Tools** menu, **Rules and Alerts**.
2. On the **E-mail Rules** tab, click **Options, Export Rules**.
3. In the **Save in** box, decide where you want the file to be stored, name the file, and click **Save, OK** until you're back in your Inbox.

If you ever need your backup, repeat the steps but click Import Rules.

📣 *If you back up a .pst file to a CD and need to use it later, before you open it in Outlook, you need to first copy the .pst to your hard drive and remove the read-only flag (you don't have to do this if the backup is saved on a CDRW). Right-click on the file and click **Properties**, untick the **Read Only** box, test the backup to make sure it works, before and after you burn the CD.*

Back Up Quick Parts

You can back up the entries you've added to Quick Parts. You'll have to find a file named NormalEmail.dotm and back it up as previously discussed.

1. Right-click the **Start** button, **Explore**. Click the folder in the Address Bar so the text in it becomes highlighted. Replace that text with *%APPDATA%\Microsoft\Templates*, and press **Enter**.
2. Find the file, **NormalEmail.dotm**, and back it up as previously discussed.

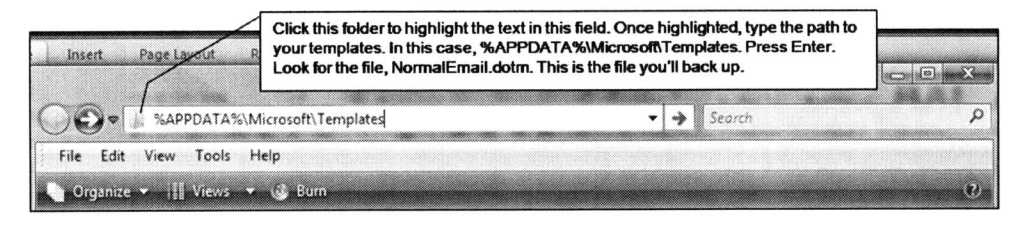

Figure 77. Find the Quick Parts file, NormalEmail.dotm, on your computer and back it up.

Move Quick Parts to a Different Computer

To move Quick Parts to a different computer, follow the instructions above and save the file, NormalEmail.dotm, to a flash drive. On the target computer, close Outlook and Word, and paste this file into the same directory, *%APPDATA%\Microsoft\Templates*, overwriting the one that's there.

Back Up Signatures

To back up or move any entries you've made to Signatures, use the same method as described for backing up Quick Parts, with one exception. You'll look for the Signatures folder (instead of the NormalEmail.dotm file). You'll find it in the same location, but it's a folder instead of a file.

📣 *If you use an online service such as MozyPro, you should include Quick Parts and Signatures in the automatic backup. See www.PeggyDuncan.com/mozypro.htm.*

STAY OUT OF TROUBLE

Just think! The moment you hit that Send button, whatever you just typed can be read around the world in a matter of seconds. The best advice I can offer you about staying out of trouble with email is to remember that it is not private.

- Network administrators can read it.
- Companies monitor it.
- Mishaps occur.
- Hackers hack it.

Company Email Policy

An email policy should be written and distributed to all employees. In addition, employees should be trained on the policy's importance and monitored to determine how well they adhere to it.

Companies should implement an email etiquette program in order to project a more professional image, increase employee productivity, and reduce liability that could derive from messages being sent that are libellous, defamatory, racist, or otherwise offensive. (Having an email etiquette program with written policies that have been signed by employees won't guarantee you'll be free of any wrongdoing in the courts. However, it will increase your favor by demonstrating you at least tried to prevent it.)

Simple Email Policy

The following sample is a short policy for companies that allow limited personal use of email.

[This document is offered by Email-policy.com. Enter your company name in the [Company] field and adapt and add rules to suit your company's needs. Note that this document is merely for informational purposes and should not be relied upon as a legal document]

[Company - Date]

Email Policy

The purpose of this policy is to ensure the proper use of [Company]'s email system. All messages distributed via the company's email system, even personal emails, are [Company]'s property. You must have no expectation of privacy in anything that you create, store, send or receive on the company's email system. Your emails can be monitored without prior notification if [Company] deems this necessary. If there is evidence that you are not adhering to the guidelines set out in this policy, the company reserves the right to take disciplinary action, including termination and/or legal action. If you have any questions or comments about this Email Policy, please contact your supervisor.

It is strictly prohibited to:

Send or forward emails containing libelous, defamatory, offensive, racist or obscene remarks. If you receive an email message of this nature, you must promptly notify your supervisor.

Forward a message or copy a message or attachment belonging to another user without acquiring permission from the originator first.

Send unsolicited email messages or chain mail.

Forge or attempt to forge email messages, or disguise or attempt to disguise your identity when sending mail.

Duty of care

Users must take the same care in drafting email as they would for any other communication. Confidential information should not be sent via email.

Personal usage

Although the company's email system is meant for business use, [Company] allows personal usage if it is reasonable and does not interfere with work.

Disclaimer

All messages will be appended with the following disclaimer: 'This message is intended only for the named recipient. If you are not the intended recipient you are notified that disclosing, copying, distributing or taking any action in reliance on the contents of this information is strictly prohibited.'

Declaration

I have read, and agree to comply with, the guidelines set out in this policy and understand that failure to do so might result in disciplinary or legal action.

Signature _____   Date _____

Printed Name _____

Extensive Email Policy

The following sample policy is extensive, and is for companies that do not allow any personal use of email.

[This document is offered by Email-policy.com. Enter your company name in the [Company] field and adapt and add rules to suit your company's needs. Note that this document is merely for informational purposes and should not be relied upon as a legal document]

[Company - Date]

Email Policy

The purpose of this policy is to ensure the proper use of [Company]'s email system and make users aware of what [Company] deems as acceptable and unacceptable use of its email system. The [Company] reserves the right to amend this policy at its discretion. In case of amendments, users will be informed appropriately.

LEGAL RISKS

Email is a business communication tool and users are obliged to use this tool in a responsible, effective and lawful manner. Although by its nature email seems to be less formal than other written communication, the same laws apply. Therefore, it is important that users are aware of the legal risks of email:

- If you send emails with any libelous, defamatory, offensive, racist or obscene remarks, you and [Company] can be held liable.
- If you forward emails with any libelous, defamatory, offensive, racist or obscene remarks, you and [Company] can be held liable.
- If you unlawfully forward confidential information, you and [Company] can be held liable.
- If you unlawfully forward or copy messages without permission, you and [Company] can be held liable for copyright infringement.
- If you send an attachment that contains a virus, you and [Company] can be held liable.

By following the guidelines in this policy, the email user can minimize the legal risks involved in the use of email. If any user disregards the rules set out in this Email Policy, the user will be fully liable and [Company] will disassociate itself from the user as far as legally possible.

Legal Requirements
The following rules are required by law and are to be strictly adhered to. It is **prohibited** to:

- Send or forward emails containing libelous, defamatory, offensive, racist or obscene remarks. If you receive an email message of this nature, you must promptly notify your supervisor.
- Forward a message without acquiring permission from the sender first.
- Send unsolicited email messages.
- Forge or attempt to forge email messages.
- Disguise or attempt to disguise your identity when sending mail.
- Send email messages using another person's email account.
- Copy a message or attachment belonging to another user without permission of the originator.

Best Practices
[Company] considers email as an important means of communication and recognizes the importance of proper email content and speedy replies in conveying a professional image and delivering good customer service. Users should take the same care in drafting email as they would for any other communication. Therefore [Company] wishes users to adhere to the following guidelines:

- **Writing emails**:
    - Write well-structured emails and use short, descriptive subjects.
    - [Company]'s email style is informal. This means that sentences can be short and to the point. You can start your email with 'Hi', or 'Dear', and the name of the person. Messages can be ended with 'Best Regards'. The use of Internet abbreviations and characters such as smileys however, is not encouraged.
    - Signatures must include your name, job title and company name. A disclaimer will be added underneath your signature (see Disclaimer)
    - Users must spell check all mails prior to transmission.
    - Do not send unnecessary attachments. Compress attachments larger than 200K before sending them.
    - Do not write emails in capitals.

- o Do not use cc: or bcc: fields unless the cc: or bcc: recipient is aware that you will be copying a mail to him/her and knows what action, if any, to take.
- o If you forward mails, state clearly what action you expect the recipient to take.
- o Only send emails of which the content could be displayed on a public notice board. If they cannot be displayed publicly in their current state, consider rephrasing the email, using other means of communication, or protecting information by using a password (see confidential).
- o Only mark emails as important if they really are important.
- **Replying to emails**:
  - o Emails should be answered within at least 8 working hours, but users must endeavor to answer priority emails within 4 hours.
  - o Priority emails are emails from existing customers and business partners.
- **Newsgroups**:
  - o Users need to request permission from their supervisor before subscribing to a newsletter or news group.
- **Maintenance**:
  - o Delete any email messages that you do not need to have a copy of, and set your email client to automatically empty your 'deleted items' on closing.

Personal Use

It is strictly forbidden to use [Company's] email system for anything other than legitimate business purposes. Therefore, the sending of personal emails, chain letters, junk mail, jokes and executables is prohibited. All messages distributed via the company's email system are [Company]'s property.

Confidential Information

Never send any confidential information via email. If you are in doubt as to whether to send certain information via email, check this with your supervisor first.

PASSWORDS

All passwords must be made known to the company. The use of passwords to gain access to the computer system or to secure specific files does not provide users with an expectation of privacy in the respective system or document.

ENCRYPTION

Users may not encrypt any emails without obtaining written permission from their supervisor. If approved, the encryption key(s) must be made known to the company.

E-MAIL RETENTION

All email messages will be deleted after 60 days. If a user has sufficient reason to keep a copy of a message, it must be moved to the folder 'For archiving'.

Email Accounts

All email accounts maintained on our email systems are property of [Company]. Passwords should not be given to other people and should be changed once a month. Email accounts not used for 60 days will be deactivated and possibly deleted.

System Monitoring

Users expressly waive any right of privacy in anything they create, store, send or receive on the company's computer system. [Company] can, but is not obliged to, monitor emails without prior notification. If there is evidence that you are not adhering to the guidelines set out in this policy, the [Company] reserves the right to take disciplinary action, including termination and/or legal action.

Disclaimer

The following disclaimer will be added to each outgoing email:
'This email and any files transmitted with it are confidential and intended solely for the use of the individual or entity to whom they are addressed. If you have received this email in error please notify the system manager. Please note that any views or opinions presented in this email are solely those of the author and do not necessarily represent those of the company. Finally, the recipient should check this email and any attachments for the presence of viruses. The company accepts no liability for any damage caused by any virus transmitted by this email.'

Questions

If you have any questions or comments about this Email Policy, please contact [Name], [Tel], [Email]. If you do not have any questions [Company] presumes that you understand and are aware of the rules and guidelines in this Email Policy and will adhere to them.

DECLARATION

I have read, understand and acknowledge receipt of the Email policy. I will comply with the guidelines set out in this policy and understand that failure to do so might result in disciplinary or legal action.

Signature:
_____   Date: _____

Printed Name:
_____

Index

A

accounts, 71
    use different signatures, 14
Activities, 49, 167
addiction, email, 24
Address Book, 162
Advanced Find, 53, 81
anagram. *See* Copy2Contact
appointments, 133
archiving. *See* AutoArchive
    open archived files, 169
Arrange By, 55
Attach Item, 90, 137
attachments
    extracting, 62
    finding messages containing, 48, 99
    open, 98
    options, 100
    preview, 98
    resize before sending, 100
    saving multiple, 99
    send calendar, 99
    send from Taskbar, 100
    sending, 99
AutoArchive, 168
AutoComplete, 78
AutoCorrect, 69
AutoCreate, 6, 117, 147
automatic formatting, 135
AutoPick, 142
autoresponders, 91

B

back up files, 169-72, *See also* AutoArchive
Bcc, 79, 162
blank calendar, 132
block message download from server, 58
Blocked Senders List
    adding to, 29
    deleting from, 30
browse the Web, 4
Building Block, 16
business card. *See* vCard

C

calendar
    add holidays, 127
    adding categories, 134
    automatic formatting, 135
    AutoPick, 142, *See* also Scheduling Assistant
    blank calendar, 132
    Calendar Overlay, 127
    change workweek, 127
    create appointment, 132, 133, 137
    create more calendars, 127
    date field, 133
    Date Navigator, 121
    define views, 122
    email it, 88
    group schedules, 143
    header and footer, 129
    moving appointments, 137
    open in new window, 126
    Page Setup, 129
    printing, 129
    private appointment, 126
    reminder, 132
    schedule resources, 144
    Scheduling Assistant, 142
    sharing, 129
    Suggested Times Pane, 142
    time field, 133
    time scale, 127
    time zone, 127
    views, 121
calendar management
    meeting alternatives, 119
    principles of, 119
Calendar Overlay, 127
carets, 92
categories, 35-40
    for calendar, 134
    for contacts, 151
    for messages, 35
    for tasks, 109
check folder size, 169

Check Full Name box, 153
clearing flagged messages, 44
color messages, 32
comments, 91
Complete, mark as, 44
completed tasks
    deleting, 113
    hiding, 111
composing messages, 65
contact linking, 139
contacts
    Activities, 49
    add from same company, 149
    add multiple phone numbers, addresses, 149
    add photo, 150
    adding categories, 152
    adding to from inside message, 150
    duplicates, removing, 155
    exporting, 155
    finding, 155, 157, 158
    flag for follow up, 158
    linking, 139, 151
    Look Up Outlook Contact, 158
    map to, 134
    organizing, 148
    other uses, 152
    receiving vCard, 165
    removing categories, 152
    sending messages to, 78, 79
    sending vCard, 102
conversation topic, 49, 50
copy Inbox folders, 11
Copy2Contact, 138, 150
Current View Pane. *See also* Navigation Pane
custom dictionary
    adding to, 22, 68
customize Quick Access Toolbar, 20
CYA folder, 11

D

data backup, 169, *See also* AutoArchive
database, 148, *See also* contacts
date field, 133
Date Navigator, 121
Define Views, 122
delay delivery, 84
Delay Send, 84

Deleted Items folder, 60, 61
    warn before deleting, 61
delivery and read receipts, 78
delivery options, 87
Dialog Box Launcher, 3
dictionary. *See* custom dictionary
disposable email address, 31
distribution lists, 159-65
    convert to Word or Excel, 165
    creating from Contacts, 160
    creating from email message, 159
    creating from scratch, 161
    delete list, 161
    delete names from message, 162
    expand, 162
    find, 162, 165
    move to new computer, 165
    printing, 165
    receiving, 165
    removing name from, 161
    restore after deleting, 161
    send messages to, 162
    sending to others, 164
    undisclosed recipients, 163
    updating, 161
Drafts folder, 6
driving directions, 134
dual monitors, 126
duplicates, removing, 155

E

edit message, 62
email accounts. *See* accounts
email addiction, 24
email big files, 96
email entire folders, 96
email etiquette, 77
email pet peeves, 71
email policies, 173
    extensive email policies, 175
    simple email policy, 174
email template, 18
emoticons, 70
empty Junk E-mail folder, 28
event, 147
Excel spreadsheet, insert, 89
export contacts, 155

F

Favorite Folders, 6, 52
Field Chooser, 54, 110
File menu, 3
finding contacts, 158
finding messages, 45-56
flagging messages, 41-45
    clearing, 44
    complete, mark as, 44
    hiding, 44
    outgoing, 42
    Set Quick Click, 42
follow up, 42
font, changing, 92
For Follow Up folder, 50
Forward, 92, 95

G

Go to Date, 147
Group By Box, 156
Group By This Field, 157
group schedules, 143

H

hidden commands, finding, 3, 4
hide flagged messages, 44
hoaxes, 76
holidays, 127
HTML
    inserting graphics, 69
hyperlink, create, 89

I

InfoBar, 44, 95
Insert
    item, 115, 138, 141
    picture, 89
Instant Search Box, 45, 48, 99
invite attendees, 140, 142
item, 115, 138, 141

J

junk email, 27-32
    Blocked Senders List, 29
    levels of protection, 28
    remove from Blocked Senders List, 30
    Safe Senders List, 31

L

linking contacts, 151
Look Up, 69

M

Mail Folders. *See also Navigation Pane*
mail merge, 82
Mailbox Cleanup, 169
mailbox size, 169
map, 134
Mark as Not Junk, 30, 31
Mark Complete. *See also tasks*
Meeting Request, 140-47
    automatic acceptance, 145
    cancel a meeting, 146
    distribution list, 146
    receiving, 146
    send update, 145
    tracking, 145
message options, 86
messages
    categorize, 35
    finding, 45-56
    forward, 92
    insert, 90
    insert calendar, 88
    insert Excel spreadsheet, 89
    insert picture, 89
    insert Word table, 89
    mail merge, 82
    Organize command, 33
    reply, 90
    reply to all, 91
    send repetitive responses, 16
    Set Quick Click, 38, 42
    sorting, 54-56
    unread, 48
    using colors, 33
Mini Toolbar, 4
monitors, using two, 126
move to folder, 62
msg, 17, 62

N

Navigation Pane, 6-9
new mail alert, 56
NormalEmail.dotm, 171
Notes, 105, 166

O

Office Assistant, 64
Office button, 3
open calendar in new window, 126
Options button, 86
Organize command, 33
organizing
    contacts, 148, 151, *See* also Copy2Contact Inbox, 10
Out of Office, 64
Outbox, 84

P

paste special, 89
pet peeves, 71
phishing, 29
pictures
    insert in a message, 69, 89, 90
    inserting in a contact, 150
printing calendar, 129
printing portion of message, 64
pst, 170

Q

Quick Access Toolbar, 4
    customizing it, 20
    moving it, 4
Quick Parts, 16
    backing up, 171
    delete entry, 17
    edit entry, 17
    moving to new computer, 172

R

read only, 171
read receipt, 78
Reading Pane, 9
rebuild search catalog, 47

recall messages, 94
recover deleted items, 61
recurring tasks, 112
reminder, 132
    change default time, 42
    Talking Alarm Clock, 132
Reply, 90, 95
    change font to black, 71
    include original message, 91
    response times, 90
    send to someone else, 78, 88
resend messages, 93
reset current view, 84, 157
resource account, 144
Ribbon
    commands, 3
    Groups, 3
    Tabs, 2
RSS Feed, 65
rules, 32-34
    assign category, 38
    back up, 171
    changing settings, 34
    edit, 34
    renaming, 34

S

Safe Senders List, 29
salutation, 67
schedule resources, 144
Scheduling Assistant, 142
Search Folders, 49-53
Send Status Report, 117
send vCard, 102
Send/Receive toolbar button, 24
sending large files, 96
sending messages to distribution lists, 162
Set Quick Click, 104
    categories, 38
    flagging, 42
    tasks, 104
shared workspace, 100
Shortcuts Navigation Pane, 8
Show in Groups, 55
signature, 13, 14
    as scripts, 17
    backing up, 172
    insert automatically, 13

switching, 15
smileys, 70
snapshot, 88
sort messages, 54-56
spam. *See* junk email
Spelling Check, 22, 68, 95
spyware, 70
subject lines, 66
    coding, 67, 120
    matching the message, 66
    writing descriptive, 66
Suggested Times Pane, 142

T

table, insert, 89
Talking Alarm Clock, 132
Task Request, 113
    accept or decline. *See also* tasks
    send to multiple people, 114
    stop updates, 114
Taskbar
    send messages from, 100
tasks
    assigning, 113
    attach email message to, 115
    attach file to, 115
    deleting completed tasks, 113
    hide completed tasks, 111
    linking contact, 109
    Mark Complete, 113
    moving to calendar, 117
    recurrence, 112
    reminder time, 42
    Set Quick Click, 104
    sort by subject, 105
    status reports, 117
    stop updates, 114
    timeline, 113
template, 18
text format, 69

Text only item, 115, 141
Thesaurus, 69
time field, 133
time scale, 127
time zone, 127, 140
timeline, 113
To-Do Bar, 5, 41, 110
    customizing, 111
    hide completed tasks, 111
    Show in Groups, 112
toolbar
    displaying, 9
tracking meeting requests, 145
typeface, 70

U

undisclosed recipients, 82, 163
unjunk, 28
unread messages stay bold, 58

V

vCard, 102, 165
    receiving, 165
    send, 102, 164
View
    change default, 24
virtual business card. *See* vCard
voting, 96

W

Who Is, 158

Y

YouSendIt Express, 96
yousendit.com, 96

www.PeggyDuncan.com   Conquer Email Overload

KEYBOARD SHORTCUTS
Outlook 2007

Message Keyboard Shortcuts – Go to Inbox (Ctrl+1)	
Check for New Mail	F5 or Ctrl+M
Create New Message	Ctrl+N (when in Mail view)
	Ctrl+Shift+M (from anywhere in Outlook)
Flag for follow-up	Ctrl+Shift+G (from within a message)
Forward Message	Ctrl+F
Move to Folder	Ctrl+Shift+V (from inside a message)
Reply to Sender	Ctrl+R (Ctrl+Shift+R is Reply All)
Save to Drafts Folder	Ctrl+S, then Esc to close
Send Message	Ctrl+Enter or Alt+S
Switch to Inbox	Ctrl+Shift+I
Switch to Outbox	Ctrl+Shift+O
Calendar Keyboard Shortcuts – Go to Calendar (Ctrl+2)	
Create New Appointment	Ctrl+N (when in Calendar)
	Ctrl+Shift+A (from anywhere in Outlook)
Open an Appointment	Double-click
Create New Meeting Request	Ctrl+Shift+Q (from anywhere in Outlook)
Accept Meeting Request	Alt+C. To decline a request Alt+D.
Go to a Date	Ctrl+G
Contact Keyboard Shortcuts – Go to Contacts (Ctrl+3)	
Create New Contact	Ctrl+N (when in Contacts)
	Ctrl+Shift+C (from anywhere in Outlook)
Create New Distribution List	Ctrl+Shift+L
Open Contacts	Ctrl+Shift+B
Task Keyboard Shortcuts – Go to Tasks (Ctrl+4)	
Create New Task	Ctrl+N (when in Tasks)
Create New Task	Ctrl+Shift+K (from anywhere in Outlook)
Create New Task Request	Ctrl+Shift+U (from anywhere in Outlook)
Other Keyboard Shortcuts	
Advanced Find	Ctrl+Shift+F
Create New Folder	Ctrl+Shift+E
Delete Message, Contact, Calendar Item, or Task	Ctrl+D or Delete key
	Shift+Delete key to bypass Deleted Items folder
Go to Folder	Ctrl+Y

www.PeggyDuncan.com   Conquer Email Overload

PEGGY DUNCAN

Peggy Duncan is an award-winning personal productivity expert, speaker, consultant, coach, and author. She travels internationally helping busy people spend less time working but get more done. In September 2009, she founded a productivity and training center, **The Digital Breakthroughs Institute**, which is located close to Atlanta's Hartsfield-Jackson International Airport (five minutes away).

Other books by Peggy include *The Time Management Memory Jogger*™, a previous book on Outlook for the 2003 version, and *Just Show Me Which Button to Click!* in *PowerPoint 2003* (currently being updated for 2007). Two ebooks include *Make Work Easy: Get Organized at Work* and *Shameless Self-Promotion: Do-It-Yourself Search Engine Optimization*. More information is at www.PeggyDuncan.com/learnmore.htm.

Peggy is an award-winning technology blogger, **www.SuiteMinute.com**. She has appeared on the TODAY show, ABC News, PBS, and Black Enterprise Business Report. Her expertise has been cited in O-The Oprah Magazine, Entrepreneur, SUCCESS, Real Simple, Health, Fitness, Black Enterprise, Self, Essence, Good Housekeeping, PINK, Positive Thinking, Woman's World, Men's Health, The New York Times, The Wall Street Journal, The Washington Post, and The International Herald Tribune.

The Durham, NC native received a BBA degree in marketing and a train the trainer certification from Georgia State University in Atlanta, Georgia. She was formally trained at IBM and was recognized by the chairman for streamlining processes that saved the company close to a million dollars a year.

Connect at 404-492-8197, worksmart@peggyduncan.com, Twitter.com/peggyduncan.

www.DigitalBreakThroughs.com

TRAINING

Yes! Peggy Duncan is available to train your team on land, at sea, and on the Web. At her place or yours.

worksmart@PeggyDuncan.com · 404-492-8197 Eastern

Instead of hiring someone who read a book or bought a CD and learned a script, hire a trainer who sits with busy people helping them figure out a better way to work. Hire someone who can help them examine and improve every aspect of how they work because she's a combination professional organizer, project manager, and computer trainer. Hire someone whose business is totally focused on helping professionals spend less time working but get more done.

Productivity

Find Time to Lead

Get Organized So You Can Think!

Spend Less Time Working but Get More Done

Technology

Computer Magic! Finish Work Six Times Quicker

Conquer Email Overload and Manage Your Time with Outlook

Create Marketing Collateral w/PowerPoint

PowerPoint All the Way (Beginning to Advanced)

Web 2.0

Do-It-Yourself Search Engine Optimization

WordPress Blogging Bootcamp

Also Offering Training Open to the Public

www.DigitalBreakThroughs.com